EXERCISE PHYSIOLOGY AS A CAREER

EXERCISE PHYSIOLOGY AS A CAREER
A Guide and Sourcebook

Tommy Boone

The Edwin Mellen Press
Lewiston•Queenston•Lampeter

Library of Congress Cataloging-in-Publication Data

Boone, Tommy.
   Exercise physiology as a career : a guide and sourcebook / Tommy Boone.
      p. cm.
   Includes bibliographical references (p.   ).
   ISBN-13: 978-0-7734-5629-7
   ISBN-10: 0-7734-5629-5
   1. Exercise--Physiological aspects--Vocational guidance. I. Title.

QP301.B578 2006
612'.044071-dc22
                                                            2006047111
hors série.

A CIP catalog record for this book is available from the British Library.

The Edwin Mellen Press   The Edwin Mellen Press
Box 450   Box 67
Lewiston, New York   Queenston, Ontario
USA 14092-0450   CANADA L0S 1L0

The Edwin Mellen Press, Ltd.
Lampeter, Ceredigion, Wales
UNITED KINGDOM SA48 8LT

Printed in the United States of America

Dedication

This book is dedicated to the students who will lead the exercise physiology profession in the 21st century with a new and relevant practice and a commanding presence in the healthcare arena.

CONTENTS

Part One

Introduction   1

Part Two

Exercise Physiology   33

Part Three

Professionalism   93

PREFACE

> In all things success depends on previous preparation and without such
> preparation there is sure to be failure. -- Confucius

This book intended to help high school and lower-division undergraduates to
make career, educational, and professional choices. It is designed to help students
evaluate career opportunities in exercise physiology. Understandably, there are a
lot of questions about careers in most fields of study. Exercise physiology is no
different, particularly at the undergraduate level. To identify the right educational
institution and faculty requires time and knowledge. Not all academic programs
that related to exercise physiology are good, and the better ones are still defining
themselves and the healthcare opportunities in exercise physiology.

Discussions about academic preparation for exercise physiologists are an
ongoing process, especially with the accreditation efforts of the *American Society
of Exercise Physiologists* (ASEP). This book is an excellent first-step in learning
about exercise physiology. It will help you to determine which academic program
is best for you. The information is presented in a straight-forward manner to
assist you, your parents, high school and college counselors, program directors
(chairs), and mentors at all levels in viewing exercise physiology as a healthcare
profession.

You will find up-to-date thinking about exercise physiology, including the
URL links to the ASEP accredited institutions. The latter is tremendously
important since it allows you direct access to the department name, the academic
degree, and the list of courses required at each institution. Also, if you are in your
first or second year of college, this guide can assist you in evaluating the different
stages of career and education development of the exercise physiology program at
your institution. You might want to compare the list of courses at your school to
the ASEP recommendation of courses and hands-on laboratory experiences for an
academic degree in exercise physiology.

The book should also be helpful to administrators, faculty, and others who are also academic advisors. Students need information about career opportunities. Faculty advisers can play an important role in getting the information to the students and their parents. Obviously, the student is ultimately responsible for making the right decisions about career options. But, what they need is accurate career information and guidance along the way. They also need information about resources, about what other skills the field of exercise physiology requires, and whether their personality matches the career.

To help in this regard, a work profile of recent graduates with an exercise physiology degree are presented to illustrate "what they do" as exercise physiologists. The profiles will also help you understand the value of an excellent education and hands-on laboratory experiences. Perhaps, most importantly, this guide should help answer your questions about different kinds of jobs, stimulate new thinking about exercise physiology as a healthcare profession, and bring attention to exactly what is exercise physiology in the 21st century and who is an exercise physiologist?

Numerous chapters include questions to encourage you to take a close look at yourself, what motivates you, and the importance of a career in healthcare. To be successful, there should be an excellent match between your own motivation in pursuing exercise physiology and the likelihood of a predictable outcome as a professional in the field. Is this what you really want to do? The answer to this question is important. Would it make a difference in your life if you could not be an exercise physiologist? If you think it would, take advantage of this book. Read it thoroughly.

Speak with other students, your teachers, friends, and guidance counselors. Check out the library, bookstore, and career center for exercise physiology books. Even though predicting the future is generally a fool's game, why not start today and get a head start on your career anyway? In looking ahead, especially from what you can learn from this book, you will be better-informed. It is far healthier and more productive to start with a solid resource, such as this book.

This book not only brings to the forefront important career opportunities in exercise physiology, it also addresses important changes within the profession. If you are interested in exercise physiology, I strongly recommend that you carefully consider the healthcare and athletic opportunities raised by Dr. Boone.

Matthew Lehn, MBA, EPC
Past President, *American Society of Exercise Physiologists*
Supervisor, Cardiopulmonary Rehabilitation
Lutheran Hospital of Indiana
Fort Wayne, IN 46818

FOREWORD

> Prevention: An ounce of it, we believe, is worth a pound of cure.
> – C. Everett Koop

From my earliest involvement in exercise physiology, prevention was always important. Perhaps, years ago there was little or no hard evidence of the cost-effectiveness of preventive measures, this is not the case today. Prevention of disease and/or dysfunction is certainly worth a pound of cure and more!

In a similar way of thinking, if exercise physiologists could prevent the continuation of yesterday's thinking that has narrowed the scope of its application to the public sector, the cure would be worth it. That is exactly the thinking of the leadership that has built the *American Society of Exercise Physiologists* (ASEP). They, too, have faced barriers in acceptance of their ideas and concepts, such as the lack of support from the academic gatekeepers.

However, the timing of the 21st century, the Internet, and the founding of the ASEP organization has changed everything. This single coming together of these three factors represents the essential information that exercise physiologists need to know that the future of exercise physiology is sound and growing. The emphasis on professional development, as the organizing framework for professional credibility and financial reward, parallels the prevention emphasis on modifying risk factors. One helps to reduce the exorbitant waste of time and energy in college and the other reduces the cost of rehabilitative and reparative medicine.

The implications of this thinking are targeted to students, parents, counselors, advisors, department chairs, and faculty are obvious. The time has come to expect that students who major in exercise physiology will graduate from an accredited program of study. The graduates will be held accountable to a code of ethics and standards of professional practice. This is important to know because the range of jobs in exercise physiology is broad and includes many that need clarification and analysis.

Hence, I urge everyone who has a career interest in health, fitness, rehabilitation, and athletics to read this book. Your efforts will result in a better understanding of the career opportunities in the profession of exercise physiology.

David K. Spierer, EdD
Assistant Professor, Sports Sciences
Long Island University, Brooklyn Campus
1 University Plaza, Room HS 303
Brooklyn, NY 11201

ACKNOWLEDGMENTS

> You need not see what someone is doing to know if it is his vocation.
> You have only to watch his eyes: A cook mixing a sauce, a surgeon
> making a primary incision...wear the same rapt expression, forgetting
> themselves in a function. – W. H. Auden

The 21st century is upon us and with it are healthcare challenges and opportunities for exercise physiologists. Thanks are in order for all exercise physiologists and others who paved the way for the shared vision of the future. A new view of exercise physiologists now integrates the study and recognition of exercise physiology independent of umbrella degree-programs like exercise science, sports science, and kinesiology.

Men and women in leadership positions have stated many times that no one can be a great leader without passion. I gratefully acknowledge the hard work and passion that the ASEP leadership has displayed on behalf of exercise physiology. The simple fact is that they have change the course of exercise physiology from a "specialist or instructor" way of thinking to a healthcare professional. Their courage and willingness to step forward when it has not always been popular to do so deserve our respect and appreciation. They know who they are and what they have done. In particular, I would like to thank Matthew Lehn, Matthew Wattles, Lonnie Lowery, Donald Diboll, Jesse Pittsley, Robert Robergs, and Todd Astorino. I give each of you my heartfelt thanks. They understand the following quote better than most: "Do what you can, with what you have, where you are." – Theodore Roosevelt

Leadership starts with action, and the ASEP leadership has seized every opportunity to ensure that something is happening within exercise physiology. Some have paid a big price for their beliefs. All of them understand and have demonstrated the self-knowledge that is so important to being a leader. Individually and collectively, each one has taken us to a new place in the history of exercise physiology. Because of what they have done, and because their actions have made a difference, the future of exercise physiology is a much better place for all of us.

Also, I would like to express my appreciation to those who are responsible for the integrity and credibility of the publishing of books at The Edwin Mellen Press. I am especially grateful to the Director, Dr. John Rupnow, for his help in bringing this book to life, and the Production Editor, Ms. Patricia Schultz.

Part One

Introduction

There is only one direction for success.

The way to success is not all at once. It is a journey. You have to work at it. The best way to begin is to start with a realistic goal, like a college education. But, you must get the right education. Choose your career path carefully. Ask questions, listen, and gamble on your hunch! If you are interested in exercise physiology, read this book. Allow yourself time to daydream about career opportunities. Remember: People do not lack intelligence; they lack will.

Chapter One

Welcome to the World of Exercise Physiology

Exercise physiologists are healthcare professionals.

It is not surprising that students are interested in exercise physiology. If you listen carefully, you can hear high school students ask questions about athletics. They are interested in the best way to train for athletics and, of course, how to build stronger muscles. College students talk about the fitness benefits of regular exercise. Psychologists are using exercise to help their patients with depression, anxiety, and stress. Other healthcare professionals, including medical doctors, physical therapists, and nurses use exercise physiologists to help their patients exercise safely and decrease body fat. Exercise physiology is a profession rich with opportunities.

The importance of exercise is bigger today than ever before. The primary reason is that exercise is central to many aspects of our lives. However, this does not mean that everyone interested in exercise understands its scientific body of knowledge or is looking to make a career of it. There are many fitness instructors in gyms and health clubs who do not have a college education, and many people who exercise regularly have careers in other fields.

Education is inevitable. The key issue from a student's perspective should be to get answers to two questions: What are the 21st century career opportunities for exercise physiologists? Which colleges are the best for preparing exercise physiologists? To answer these questions correctly, students need accurate and unbiased information to help

> **Exercise is bigger today than ever before.**

them make the right career choice, whether it is doing research in exercise physiology or working in a hospital cardiac rehab program.

Unfortunately, the world of exercise physiology is mixed with fitness instructors who are not academically qualified. They do not have the right core competencies. As a result, they can do more harm than good. This is why your parents or friends should be especially careful when hiring a personal trainer. There is no way of knowing for sure that the person is qualified. In fact, given the need to understand the multifaceted issues that underpin human anatomy and physiology, the trainer who wants to do the right thing may not know how to do it safely. Yet, increasingly, whether it is a medical doctor, researcher, supplement company representative, or a pastor at your church, someone always has something to say about life's secrets to staying healthy by exercising.

The signs of misinformation are familiar to every professionally prepared exercise physiologist. Torn or overused muscles, a negative attitude towards exercise, overuse injuries, or an inappropriate competitive spirit that threatens the safety of the participant is all too common. Professional exercise physiologists understand these are signs of misinformation and poor judgment. Often, the problem is not the individual who is trying to lose weight or get stronger, but the failure of the instructor or personal trainer to engage the use of exercise appropriately and safely.

Many of these individuals have not had an adequate education in the scientific principles of training. Much of what they teach is what worked for them. It does not matter if they were athletes or even if they look good. The question is: "Do they

> **Exercise physiologists are professionals in health, fitness, rehabilitation, and athletics.**

have a college education in exercise physiology?" Are they board certified to guide the training and development of clients and athletes?

Of course this does not mean that hard work and personal experiences are not important. Undoubtedly, there are a few excellent personal trainers who did not attend college. But, in general, the problem is that not having a college education encourages the likelihood of making mistakes. No one should have to

4

be subjected to a person's instructions to run faster, get bigger, or stronger who is not a college graduate.

This is why all exercise physiologists must attend college. Rather than expose clients to a "new or never heard of strength building exercise," exercise physiologists use proven and acceptable techniques and procedures to build and strengthen the musculoskeletal system. Hence, it is always in the best interest of the client to ask the following questions: "Where did you do your academic training? Are you an ASEP board certified exercise physiologist?" This is also why graduating from an accredited exercise physiology program is the right path to professional credibility.

Exercise physiologists are academically prepared to teach clients how to be healthier through regular exercise. They understand strength development and fitness practices. Their education has also provided them the understanding of safety principles to avoid cardiovascular complications. Professional training and leadership practices are integrated with course content and hands-on laboratory experiences. They understand that it is complicated and challenging to make major changes in a person's lifestyle.

Disease and dysfunction influence everyone in some way or another. No one wants to be misled and no one should be. This is why it is no longer acceptable that anyone with a good physical appearance is automatically considered a knowledgeable exercise professional.

> Accountability ultimately resides in the individual, but begins with a professionally credible academic program of study.

Remember: Regardless of the trainer's appearance, is the trainer academically qualified to lead clients in fitness development and positive steps towards

ASEP is the professional organization of exercise physiologists.

better health. The public benefits from academic knowledge and scientific advances by proven professionals, just as it does from credible doctors versus quacks.

The good news is that the board certified exercise physiologists passed the test of sound academic knowledge and scientific thinking. They are stewards of sound and safe practices of health, wellness, fitness, rehabilitation, and athletics. This thinking got its start within the professional infrastructure of the *American Society of Exercise Physiologists* (ASEP) and the definition of exercise physiology. This is an important understanding since ASEP is "the" professional organization of exercise physiologists as healthcare professionals [1].

This Book and Your Future

| The times they are a changin'. – Bob Dylan

This book highlights many of the good things about exercise physiology, including its academic parts. Students considering a healthcare career in exercise physiology should know about the professional opportunities, salaries, code of ethics, board certification, and the exercise physiologist's scope of practice. A thorough understanding of each is important to making the right career decision.

For decades, exercise physiologists used the principles and theories of science and statistics to solve human-related problems through research. For decades, exercise physiology was viewed primarily in terms of research only. Today, exercise physiologists are applying their findings to practical health and fitness issues and concerns. They still use laboratory procedures to achieve the best results, interpret data, and devise solutions to problems that face clients (including athletes). But, as the profession is changing, so are the roles of exercise physiologists and the places in which they work. Career opportunities for exercise physiologists are expanding. Not only is exercise used to improve fitness and quality of health, society's attitude towards exercise is much improved over yesterday's thinking.

> **Exercise physiologists are healthcare professionals.**

Increasingly, exercise physiologists are developing exercise prescriptions for clients of other healthcare professionals. They work with other healthcare professionals studying the human body. Many assist scientists who conduct human research. They help to collect and analyze physiological data, or they may develop individualized exercise prescriptions to manage healthcare concerns. They are usually concerned with cost containment that is shaping the healthcare industry and, therefore, are giving more attention to preventive care. In this capacity, exercise physiologists are helping to reduce the potential cost of medical services by reshaping not only the nature of healthcare but the way in which healthcare is provided.

The purpose of this book is to provide reliable, up-to-date, relevant, and detailed career information for aspiring exercise physiologists. The content is written to help you think about important career questions such as:

1. What is exercise physiology?
2. Who is an exercise physiologist?
3. What are the required career preparation?
4. What are the required laboratory skills and experiences?
5. What kinds of equipment and instrumentation do they use?
6. What are the required certifications?
7. Where are they employed?
8. What are they paid?

Answers to these questions are critical to a successful beginning and work in the profession of exercise physiology. This book will help set the stage for that beginning. Achieving success is important for obvious reasons. Students want to be successful. After all, many students are paying for their own college tuition through regular academic loans.

Compared with other healthcare professions, such as physical therapy, occupational therapy, and nursing, and where they are today with licensure and professional autonomy, exercise physiologists must constantly entertained new ideas and views and professional accountability. This is why this book is so important. If you are thinking of an engaging scientific career like exercise

7

physiology, now is the time to read this book. Remember, the goal is to make the right career choice. Now is the time to ask the right questions. Now is the time to determine if exercise physiology is the right career choice for you.

Exercise physiologists help clients and others understand how to build muscle and decrease body fat, and how to do so safely. Others help clients figure

> **Do you have a strong desire to help improve people's lives?**

out how to commit to finding the time to exercise regularly. Still others help patients with cardiac disease or other life-threatening diseases get the right amount (intensity and duration) of exercise. Exercise physiologists often provide professional services in hospital-related settings. Others work in community-based lifestyle management facilities.

> **Are you interested in the business of healthcare?**

Exercise physiologists own their own facilities, whereby they conduct research and provide exercise testing, cardiovascular assessment, and rehabilitation services and assistance to improve the physical and psychological functioning of children, athletes of all ages, as well as their parents to maximize health, performance, and well-being. It is increasingly likely that more students will want to think of exercise physiology in business terms.

If you are a high school student, this book will help you identify the science courses that should be taken prior to attending college. You may want to speak to an exercise physiologist to discuss strength and conditioning types of jobs. Be sure to ask the following questions. How many athletes do

> **How about the business of athletics?**

they work with in any given day? How many meetings do they attend weekly? How do they handle emergencies? How often do they travel to visit other clients or to attend conferences?

One way to find answers to these questions is to contact a local college or university and ask to meet with the chair of the department. Indicate that you are interested in learning more about exercise physiology and the career options. Ask

8

if you can meet with an exercise physiologist who has an interest in something you like (e.g., strength and conditioning, research or, perhaps, rehabilitation).

Ask the exercise physiologist to explain the differences between exercise science and exercise physiology. Ask about the laboratories and hands-on opportunities for students. While at the university, take a moment to discuss the *American Society of Exercise Physiologists* (ASEP) with the faculty.

http://www.asep.org

Although the ASEP organization has the infrastructure in place, there is still much to be done. Numerous challenges await further development, especially the revision of the ASEP Standards of Professional Practice [2]. There also remains much to be learned about working with professionals in the established healthcare settings. The challenges, benefits, and application of different kinds of research to the public sector need study and clarification. Clearly, there are many career opportunities yet to be thoroughly evaluated in health, fitness, rehabilitation, and athletics.

Of course, the question you need answered is this: "Is exercise physiology for you?" For a variety of reasons, it could be. Are you are interested a supervisory or administrative position? If so, these positions usually require an advanced degree (such as the master's degree). College and university teaching positions and most research appointments usually require the doctorate degree. As much as I would like to state it otherwise, the only way to know whether exercise physiology is for you is to give this book a thorough reading.

Making a Difference

Healthcare should not be viewed as separate from the services of exercise physiologists.

The exercise physiology body of knowledge has made a difference in how the public views the profession. It is scientifically-based and recognized by healthcare professionals worldwide. With the rapid growth in aging in the United

States, exercise is becoming a central component to stabilizing and/or rehabilitating disease and dysfunction. Opportunities are excellent for exercise physiologists with an interest in private practice. Many career opportunities in the foreseeable future will stem from the need to retain and/or develop the nation's health and fitness. This is especially the case since many hospitals continue to limit the length of patient stays, and hospital costs continue to rise.

Exercise physiologists can make a big difference in healthcare. This means that they will have increased employment opportunities. Employment for exercise physiologists with backgrounds in gerontology will become increasingly an important career option, given the growing numbers of assisted-living and senior-living communities. In other words, the expanding senior population will stimulate a big demand for credible professionals with a scientific understanding of the physiological adjustments and adaptations that result from regular exercise.

Most exercise physiologists will want you to know that exercise physiology is not just a job. It is a professional career. They believe that their specialized body of knowledge can make a difference in the quality of life of every person. Regular exercise is important to almost all facets of life. For certain, it is much easier to maintain lean muscle tissue when engaged

> **Exercise physiology is a healthcare profession.**

in regular exercise than when inactive. Also, exercise promotes positive mental health and emotional stability. Thus, exercise physiologists have the opportunity to make a real difference in designing and managing lifestyle of clients.

Professional Careers

> We must learn the importance of sharing risk in healthcare issues. And, in so doing, we must learn to express ownership of our work.

As you can see, a career in exercise physiology can mean many careers in one. This is true because exercise physiology is a collective body of many academic subjects with important healthcare implications. Given the diversity of health and

10

fitness concerns across different age groups (children vs. elderly) and different levels of sports training (recreational vs. athletic), there is the opportunity to specialize.

> **Biomechanics Anatomy Physiology Psychology Statistics Nutrition Rehabilitation ECG Research**

Exercise physiologists lead, instruct, and motivate individuals and groups in exercise activities, including but not limited to:

1. cardiovascular training
2. strength and muscular development training,
3. range of motion (flexibility) training.

These activities are carried out in commercial and not-for-profit health clubs, resorts, and homes. This means that a career in exercise physiology is never dull, especially when working with special

> **There are career opportunities to suit every personality.**

populations that can be helped by regular exercise (e.g., diabetic patients, heart patients, obesity patients, depressed patients, and cancer patients).

Increasingly, exercise physiologists are found in workplaces, where they organize and direct health and fitness lifestyle management programs for employees of all ages. They help clients assess their physical fitness and set goals to improve aerobic capacity, decrease body fat, and a mix of other activities. Not only do they work in the clinical settings, such as in a public or private hospital, they can also choose to work in private practice, academic institutions, research settings, and health promotion facilities.

Board certified exercise physiologists often work in conjunction with other health professionals who are either directly or indirectly associated with careers in law, psychology, and marketing. One of the most attractive aspects of a career in exercise physiology is the demand in athletics. Often times, this

11

involves creating and maintaining training programs that meet the needs of the athletes, including cardiovascular and muscular assessments.

Exercise physiologists may also want to work in companies that manufacture fitness and testing equipment. Or, they want to coordinate the training of injured athletes or supervise the hiring and training of fitness staff at the corporate level.

As an exercise physiologist, you can provide the care and professional know-how to make a real difference in an athlete's life and in the lives of others.

> **Exercise physiologists make a real difference in an athlete's life and physical performance.**

Only a few other healthcare professionals have the scientific background and education to offer the diversity and depth of knowledge and skills required to care for and supervise athletes and members of the public.

Chapter Two

This Book is for YOU: More Help!

Finding a career is a complicated process. Books help, and it can be argued that a good book helps to make it less complicated.

Throughout history, many books have been written for many different reasons. This book reveals the different kinds of jobs and hands-on skills performed by exercise physiologists in the public sector. It describes the academic preparation required of exercise physiology students before they sit for the ASEP board certification exam to practice as an exercise physiologist.

Whether you are a student with questions about exercise physiology or you have a friend who has an interest in exercise physiology, this book can help you. Whether you are a guidance counselor working with high school seniors, an academic advisor, or a parent who is giving advice to a college student, this book will help answer important questions about the academic course work, hands-on lab skills, and training of exercise

> **Counselors, advisors, parents, students, and exercise physiologists can benefit from the different chapters in this book.**

physiologists, as well other important qualifications. Anyone interested in this field should understand the academic requirements of the 21st century exercise physiologist and their professional healthcare services.

This book will also help you understand what is meant by the exercise physiology body of knowledge, the importance of research, and why exercise physiologists place such a high value on critical thinking and research skills. You will become

> **Why is academic accreditation important, and is the exercise physiology major accredited?**

familiar with different issues in the field, especially the professional development and ethical concerns that face the profession. The purpose is to provide information on topics that are consistent with your questions and concerns about the profession. For example, you need answers to the following questions:

1. What types of courses do exercise physiology students take?
2. Are academic majors in exercise physiology accredited?
3. Do exercise physiologists have licensure?
4. Why is exercise physiology a healthcare profession?
5. Is there a code of ethics?

If you are informed and can answer these questions, you will feel more comfortable about a career in exercise physiology. If you believe the opportunity to work with people of all ages is worthwhile and personally satisfying, you will enjoy a career in exercise physiology. There are many different career opportunities and entrepreneurial possibilities, but you need sound advice to make the right decision.

What You Also Need to Know

Now that you understand a few of the important questions to ask, this book will help you, in particular, to understand that exercise science is not exercise physiology. Imagine how good you will feel knowing that you did not make the mistake of majoring in "exercise science" thinking it was "exercise physiology." After all, why would you want to pay tuition for an academic major that is not career-driven?

> The best way to predict the future is to create it. -- Peter Drucker

It is also logical that you would want to know whether the academic institution and/or department you are considering support the "Exercise Physiologist Certified" (EPC) exam to practice exercise physiology [1]. There may even be concern whether an academic major requires an internship with supervised hands-on experiences before the right to practice independently.

14

Another consideration is the academic course work. In addition to the scientific courses such as: (1) kinesiology (or anatomy); (2) physiology of exercise; (3) sports biomechanics; (4) electrocardiography and/or graded exercise testing; (5) exercise nutrition; and (6) cardiac rehabilitation, does the academic major require students to take courses in management, business, and accounting? Do they have the opportunity to take courses that will help them understand health concerns that associate with childhood obesity and the aging baby boomers? Obviously, one only has to listen to the evening news to understand that both have important health implications.

This book will identify the jobs that require more personalized service to keep clients motivated and healthy. Health clubs, for example, are promising but your ability to launch the right career depends on a number of factors at graduation. Employers look for graduates with good

> **What do you have to offer the employer? Are you a critical thinker? Do you have a positive attitude?**

work habits, good communication skills, regular attendance, punctuality, and a positive attitude.

Employers look to hire responsible and well-educated graduates. They want to know whether the graduates can perform their duties in a responsible and dependable manner, which raises several questions:

- Are you interested in the strengthening your communication skills?
- Are you cultivating the skills you need to create solutions?
- Do you have the discipline needed for tackling tough problems?

Scientific Thinking is Also Important

The scientific principles of human anatomy and physiology are important to understanding the musculoskeletal system or when interpreting an athlete's maximal oxygen uptake test (VO_2 max). In fact, it is next to impossible to evaluate athletes and not have a thorough knowledge of the VO_2 max test. What

15

does the VO_2 max test really measure? What are the criteria for reaching the maximum capacity for aerobic metabolism during exercise? Exercise physiologists are interested in these questions and others like them because they help to define an important area of study and research [2].

You may want to study the role of the respiratory system, the circulatory system, the musculoskeletal system, or the endocrine system during exercise or the use of "exercise as medicine." Later, you may want to study the benefits of

Exercise is better than medicine!

regular physical activity for patients with coronary artery disease (CAD) and whether the benefit is psychological or physiological. Still later, you may want to research the mechanisms of exercise and its effect on cancer, diabetes, cystic fibrosis, and pulmonary diseases and how exercise physiologists are involved in finding answers to health related diseases and/or dysfunctions.

Scientific thinking is not easy, but it can be learned. It takes a lot of work, practice, and mentoring. This is why exercise physiologists have learned to raise questions, collect and analyze data, and think open-mindedly about the implications of their findings. Critical thinking is, in short, an important part of the education of exercise physiologists. As

Exercise physiologists make a living by thinking straight.

a result, straight thinking is more than a motto; it is a professional way of maintaining integrity.

16

Chapter Three

Counselors, Exercise Physiologists, and Others

Counselors have been and always will be critical for many students in finding the right career.

High school and college students seek careers in the healthcare field for many reasons. Some students may have specific goals in mind, such as working in a hospital or healthcare center. Others may have family members or friends who work in healthcare and have come to like what they do. Still others may have experienced an injury and have enjoyed the patient-client relationship that sparked an interest in working with patients.

Increasingly, more students are interested in teaching at the college or university level. They want to teach, do research, and publish scientific papers. Perhaps, a college teacher convinced the students during a visit to his laboratory that research could be fun and a rewarding experience. Some may have heard that heart patients benefit from exercise rehabilitation, as do cancer patients and diabetic patients. Perhaps, they have been encouraged by a family member or their medical doctor to use exercise to lower borderline high blood pressure.

Why Exercise Physiology?

Athletes are especially interested in exercise physiology.

Athletes want to know more about how to train the body. They want to run faster, jump higher, and develop bigger muscles. They are motivated by the opportunity to work with the cardiovascular and metabolic equipment in the exercise physiology laboratory. They like the idea of measuring strength, range of motion, and assessing the endurance potential of the cardiovascular system.

Good students ask questions.

Some athletes want to know more about how the exercise physiology body of knowledge was developed through research and statistical methods. Often times, they have an interest in the prevention and/or rehab of psycho-physiological diseases and metabolic dysfunctions. They may also want to help shape the public health agenda towards better health and wellness policies.

The role of parents, guidance counselors, college faculty, and others in helping high school and college students choose the right career path has been recognized for decades. What has been missing is a book written specifically to help students determine the right career path. Now, parents, counselors, and faculty members have the content they need to share with students. Questions that deal with wages, job market trends, skills for different types of work, and the advancement opportunities are described in this book.

What is a typical salary for exercise physiologists?

Information about job satisfaction and salary is always important. Students need to know the factors that help to ensure job satisfaction in different work environments. This point is critical, given that only about one-half of the employees in society are said to be satisfied with their work. Finding meaningful work is important and, therefore, should be planned for accordingly.

Where do exercise physiologists work?

Parents, counselors, and others can help by encouraging students to evaluate their personal values, communication skills, and abilities. For example, if they value teaching and have critical thinking skills, they may enjoy a career in teaching. Other careers are found in the health and wellness industry, clinical and rehabilitation programs, and in the military government for those who want to work directly with clients.

Then, too, there are excellent opportunities in the "business" side of healthcare. Students who are inclined to be self-employed should interview people in their work environment. Many employers are happy to talk about their work. Job shadowing is a valuable way to learn about different career options in the private sector and whether a person has any interest in doing the same kind of work.

Some graduates have started their own healthcare business that caters to health, wellness, and fitness issues and concerns. They enjoy the administrative aspects of the work while not being accountable to an employer. Often, while working alongside side other healthcare professionals, they develop an interest in the management of disease from the business perspective [1].

- **Making the Right Decision**

> **Selecting the right career opportunity requires an understanding of exercise physiology.**

While opportunities are numerous, there are many differences among jobs that are unique to each career option. If you are a counselor, parent, teacher, or a friend, your success in helping students plan for a career in exercise physiology is directly linked to your understanding of "what is exercise physiology" and "what exercise physiologists do in the public sector."

Generally speaking, students are excited about measuring physiological responses like heart rate and blood pressure. Helping students find access to an exercise physiologist so that they can ask questions about the laboratory equipment is helpful. They will want to know how exercise physiologists are involved in sports and athletics, especially in helping athletes train better and more efficiently.

Once again, some graduates will want be self-employed and, thus they will need specific information about how to set up and manage a business oriented to athletes. If you are in position to help, the students will benefit greatly. If not, point the students to the ASEP web pages. One in particular that will be especially helpful is the PEPonline electronic journal entitled *Professionalization of Exercise Physiologyonline*:

19

Guidance Counselors

It is very important that students and their parents speak with high school and college guidance counselors. They are professionals with a strong commitment to helping students. Also, they have answers to most questions regarding college majors. Equally important, they know the questions to ask in determining which career will satisfy the educational needs of

> **Most college counselors know the exercise physiologists on their college campus.**

individual students. They will set up an appointment to speak with the chair of the department and/or individual faculty members.

Counselors, therefore, need to know the academic essentials of different programs of study. If they are new at their job, this book will help them understand exercise physiology. As an example, they need to know which academic institutions offer an accredited academic major in exercise physiology. They need to know the differences between a major in kinesiology or human performance with a concentration in exercise science and the academic major in exercise physiology.

This book will help counselors without wasting their time or energy. Copies of this book should be in the bookstores of all academic institutions. Students, counselors, and parents should have access to the book. They can use it to identify questions that need answers to, such as:

- Have you visited an exercise physiology department to ask questions about course work, credentials (certification), and hands-on laboratory opportunities/
- Have you observed an exercise physiology professor teaching or doing research?
- Have you talked with an academic advisor in exercise physiology?

20

- Have you talked with a college teacher about exercise physiologists who work in the public sector?
- Have you thought about the day-to-day activities of working with athletes, adults in fitness programs, or heart patients in hospital settings?
- Do you know the salary ranges for exercise physiologists in different careers within exercise physiology?
- Are you willing to consider going to graduate school after the completion of the undergraduate degree in exercise physiology?
- Are you comfortable with the application of exercise physiology concepts in the non-academic world of business as a self-employed, independent professional?
- Do you have a strong personal need to maintain your own health and fitness, and do you have the same need to help others?

Exercise Physiologists

This book can also be used as a text in the "Introduction to Exercise Physiology" course. It is conveniently divided into chapters that provide specific information for students and professors. Students need to know the following [2]:

- What does an exercise physiologist do?
- What is the professional practice of exercise physiology?
- What is the exercise physiologist's salary range for different types of jobs and/or academic preparation?

Answers to these questions can help students understand the ASEP effort to establish exercise physiology as a healthcare profession, especially the autonomy of their own practice. Exercise physiologists can share with students the rationale for a professional organization. They can discuss the course work in exercise physiology, the importance of professionalism and credibility, and the movement towards licensure.

Science-oriented students as well as students interested in sports will have diverse personal and academic backgrounds. They are not all alike by any means. Most have different reasons for considering exercise physiology as a

| Why is professionalism important? |

major. A certain number will have no idea why professionalism is important or what it has to do with sports training [3]. Understanding why a student wants to major in exercise physiology is critical to helping the student make the right decision. Helping students understand the perseverance needed to complete years of scientific and technical laboratory work is important, too. Students should be encouraged to:

1. Make a list of reasons why exercise physiology is an interesting academic area of study and, then, make a list of reasons why it is not.
2. Identify at least two exercise physiologists and ask them about their work and what they did to get to where they are today.

Program Directors

Students should speak with the program director (also called chairperson) to discuss the pros and cons of different academic majors. They might not think they have access to the director, but they do.

| Ask for an appointment with the director to talk about a career in exercise physiology. |

Directors can help students think through different career options and whether a career in exercise physiology is right for them. It is an excellent way of getting at new insights and ideas to guide students and to promote a relationship between the administration and students.

Chapter Four

So YOU want to be an Exercise Physiologist

Imagine where you will be, and it will be so. - Gladiator

If you were to tell your friends that you plan to attend college, what would they say? Perhaps, they would ask the following questions: "Which college are you planning to attend? What are you going to major in? Have you thought about the tuition costs?" Today, the average tuition charge (before aid and grants) for the

> **Have you thought about the tuition costs to attend college?**

majority of full-time undergraduates at a public university (four-year, BA-granting) is $8,000 per year. Approximately 40% of the full-time undergraduates (before student aid) face tuition charges of $5,000 per year. At a private college or university, the tuition is closer to $21,000 per year. Clearly, most college students will pay back thousands of dollars in tuition charges to loan institutions.

Of course, students who choose to live on campus pay room and board fees that often range from $6,000 to $8,000 on average. There may also be special fees for laboratory or computer use. These charges do not take into consideration transportation and books. The "expected family contribution" may not be sufficient to offset the price of college. Hence, students benefit from the low interest rates on federal loans as well as the possibility of federal tuition tax benefits available to families with low to middle incomes.

Since it is clear that a large percent of all bachelor degree recipients graduate with student loan debt, why do young people want to go to college? Part of the reason is that the average income of full-time workers with a college degree is close to 50% higher than the worker with a high school diploma. Now, imagine this, a young lady says: "I plan to go to college to be an exercise physiologist."

She knows that it will cost money to attend college, and that it will be a lot of work, but going to college is exactly what she wants to do.

Also, consider this: What if her parents started saving $100 per month when she was born? At 5% interest, they would have saved more than $17,000 when she is ready to start college. With the savings, they make it easier for their daughter to attend college. What if both parents have a formal postsecondary education? In other words, one might conclude that she has not only been encouraged to develop good study habits but her parents have very likely spent considerable time discussing career opportunities.

When children and high school students are encouraged to aim high, explore all their options, and plan for a higher education, it is easier to understand their interest in getting a college or university degree. Similarly, when a person says, "I have thought about it a lot, and I want to be an exercise physiologist. That person may very well have been influenced by a guidance counselor who helped to map out a college preparatory curriculum. No wonder the person is motivated to make the right decision. No wonder that person is taking physics, advanced math, science, chemistry, and biology courses during her senior year in high school.

College is about many things. What is not so obvious is the importance of learning how to be a critical thinker. If you are one of the many high school or college students interested in research findings about staying healthy, then exercise physiology is likely to make an enormous difference in your life. Students will learn how to develop critical thinking skills, and the importance of a healthy skepticism. Also, they will learn that the **Exercise physiologists are** structure of exercise physiology is being reshaped **critical thinkers.** by new challenges and opportunities.

So, if you are interested in planning, studying, and investing thousands of dollars to be an exercise physiologist, you need to know that becoming an exercise physiologist has its challenges and demands. You must be willing to work hard to realize your dreams and, if you are careful in selecting the right academic program of study, you will become what you imagine in your mind and heart.

The Professional Organization

There is only one credible exercise physiology professional. That person is either someone who graduates from an accredited exercise physiology academic major or who is successful in passing the "Exercise Physiologist Certified" (EPC) examination.

> **The heart of exercise physiology is its professional organization.**

• The ASEP leaders consider exercise physiology a healthcare profession with strong scientific training in athletics. The leadership [1] acknowledges and supports the ASEP professional infrastructure. They and the members are responsible for upholding the integrity of the professional title, Exercise Physiologist, and the profession's standards of practice.

The ASEP standards represent a major opportunity to make a difference. They define what exercise physiologists do in healthcare and athletics. Hence, members of the public sector interested in improving their fitness, health and wellness can go to an exercise physiologist for guidance and supervision. This is also why some academic programs have forged partnerships with management and business departments for students who want a career in the "business" side of exercise physiology.

Whereas in the past exercise physiologists tended to develop career paths opportunistically (i.e., in the gyms and where they could find a job), high school graduates entering college today and even more so in the future will create their own career paths matched by a commensurate financial reward system. The increased recognition as healthcare professionals and the specialization in athletics are encouraging, important, and a legitimate means of financial stability.

In addition to the pressures within society to look at healthcare differently, the ASEP leadership has defined new and significant opportunities for exercise physiologists in healthcare. Of course, there are still many opportunities for work as faculty members, researchers, and administrators in a variety of roles that interact with health and athletics.

If you like working with athletes or if you believe you can help change the lifestyle of individuals who need professional support and guidance to reduce risk factors for disease and dysfunction, and if you understand the importance of participating in scientific discourse, then exercise physiology, the ASEP organization, and board certification should be of interest to you.

Career Options in Business

Exercise physiology has spawned a strong interest in the business of healthcare. Increasingly, there are business opportunities for exercise physiologists who are interested in creating new health and fitness programs, new wellness and rehabilitation policies and procedures and, in particular, new thinking about handling obesity, stress, and tension.

Leaders have created a shared culture and values that encourage new career opportunities that are not

> Like medicine, exercise physiology is a diverse profession, ranging from athletics to exercise prescriptions for heart patients.

only emotionally and intellectually rewarding, but also financially rewarding. This is why students are attracted to the idea of creating their own exercise physiology healthcare center. And, increasingly, more educational programs require students to take elective courses in business and management.

Preparing students for the changing context of what they will do in the

> Exercise physiology career paths will continue to evolve for decades to come.

public sector with an ever increasing care for clients requires an understanding of professional autonomy in community settings and a continuing professional education to update

knowledge as it develops. At all levels of the student's education, there will be increased attention paid to critical thinking and the implications to curriculum design. Students will use critical thinking skills to acquire knowledge in ways that will facilitate client care, whether that person is an athlete or an obese patient with diabetes [2]. They will use computer driven technology and statistical information linked to healthcare issues and concerns that are improved through regular exercise.

The interaction of events both in health and athletics will influence decisions about exercise physiology that will continue to impact the education process. Political factors will likely interact with economic concerns in faculty decisions about exercise physiology, core courses in the curriculum, elective courses in and outside of the department, and accreditation of academic programs.

Students with an interest in exercise physiology should be aware of these considerations when deciding on the right career path. Perhaps, it is also important to appreciate, regardless of a graduate's first big job, that the average person in the United States holds nine jobs between the ages of 18 and 34 (according to the National Longitudinal Survey of Youth; a survey conducted by the U.S. Bureau of Labor Statistics). Here is my point: While recent graduates may start out as program fitness managers, they will acquire other titles, more responsibilities, and higher salaries.

Exercise physiology is no different from other careers in the healthcare industry. Professional respect, job security, and medical and life insurance benefits are important when considering which career path to take. Part of the role of the faculty, advisors, and counselors is to help students understand the importance of their decisions and the impact of each on their lives for a long time. Seldom is any one job or even the responsibilities of a

Employees must commit to lifelong learning to keep abreast with new academic and hands-on skills.

particular job going to stay the same. Without a crystal ball to look into, certainty is elusive at best. However, in terms of cardiac rehabilitation and athletics, the take home message is that neither is likely to remain the exclusive focus for exercise physiology practice.

Most evidence points to a high probability that exercise physiologists will become increasingly more interactive and involved with new technology. This means more graduates will need to be adaptable and flexible, as well as technically proficient in the face of expanding the practice of exercise physiology. This is also why educational renewal within established academic programs is an important part of the transition from exercise science to exercise physiology.

There are many additional questions that will require thoughtful responses from the exercise physiology community, both students and faculty. As an example, how can the Internet be helpful in writing resumes and letters of intent? How can faculty integrate more successfully the use of physiological technologies and technical information in the teaching of exercise physiology? How can students plan for interview opportunities? The key point is that the challenges ahead for exercise physiology and the educational process are numerous.

You may want to analyze the current job market salary ranges and career opportunities. Think 5 to 10 years ahead. Think about your strengths and the role of each in being successful in exercise physiology. Why not develop a career plan or write an essay that describes the role of exercise physiology as a healthcare profession. Talk with graduates of a local university about areas of specialization within exercise physiology.

To adapt more readily, students need a sense of the "big picture" within exercise physiology, healthcare, and athletics. That perspective may best be supplied by volunteering time to shadow an exercise physiologist in your area of interest.

Advice from Advisors and Counselors

So you are convinced that being an exercise physiologist is a great idea. Now you are asking yourself, "What should I concentrate on doing while in college or even before going to college?" As mentioned earlier, it is always best to attend an accredited program.

There are also other academic paths to a career in exercise physiology. For example, you could attend an academic program that is not accredited by the *American Society of Exercise Physiologists*. Such programs offer undergraduate degrees in a variety of areas, including kinesiology, human performance, and exercise science to mention three of some 30 different degree titles [3] None of these academic programs can graduate an exercise physiologist.

But, if the programs offer a significant number of exercise physiology core courses such as exercise physiology, kinesiology, sports biomechanics, exercise and sports nutrition, cardiac rehabilitation, cardiovascular physiology, exercise prescription, and research and, if the students are required to do an internship prior to graduation, then, following graduation, you can sit for the EPC exam. If you pass the written and hands-on laboratory parts of the exam, the Board of Certification (housed within *The Center for Exercise Physiology-online*) will allow for an exception in which you can refer to yourself as an "Exercise Physiologist."

When students ask questions about career paths in exercise physiology, the following advice is recommended for advisors and counsels:

1. Identify a college that offers an academic degree in exercise physiology that is accredited. Such programs should automatically offer the right combination of science prerequisites, exercise physiology core courses, and hands-on experiences to ensure that passing the EPC exam is a high probability.
2. Go to the college and sit in several exercise physiology classes and, if possible, attend a laboratory session, too.
3. Do some volunteer work at the gym, corporate fitness center, or cardiac rehabilitation program or hospital.

How Can Professors Help?

Students should make an effort to determine the interest their professors have in teaching and research. Professors who are not interested in teaching cannot help you learn how to think. Find a department where the professors are "teachers," and where there is the opportunity to learn by getting

> **Students should make the effort to get to know the professors who teach the exercise physiology courses.**

involved in hands-on experiences.

Look for academic opportunities for integrated learning, particularly when it comes to understanding and applying cardiovascular physiology. As with most areas of study, you usually get out of the programs what you put into them. Of course, your chances of success are better when the teachers are committed to a mind-set that is geared to helping students. Changing a teacher's interest from research to teaching is not easy.

As time permits, but certainly earlier than later, meet one-on-one with your professors. Excellent teachers do not take students for granted. It is also important that students know what their teachers think about exercise physiology. Is it a research discipline or is it a healthcare profession? Keep in mind that not only large research institutions, but professors in the smallest colleges can get enmeshed with research.

Students should network with their teachers and others who might have an influence on their learning and intellectual curiosity. This is an important recommendation for students in the healthcare field, where interdependence among professionals is important to the welfare of the client.

Laboratory Opportunities

Laboratory opportunities are extremely important for students. Students must get involved in data collection and analysis. It helps them to better understand the physiology of the body. Otherwise, students are left to memorize numbers from a text. The laboratory experiences cannot be something that is available only for graduate students.

If you find that you have a particular interest (e.g., the physiology of track performances), then speak with your advisor or professor. Ask if he or she could help or whether there is funding to do a laboratory project. Of course, it is always possible to offer your services as a subject for someone else's study. Keep your eyes and ears open and discuss the research that you have read with your friends, students, and teachers.

Potential employers are always interested in your ability to read and interpret research findings. Analysis of oxygen consumption (VO_2 max), that is,

> **Most academic institutions have metabolic carts for physiological assessments.**

the energy expended during exercise, is always an excellent area to research. Exercise physiology laboratories also have percent body fat analyzers, muscle strength and endurance equipment, bicycles and treadmills, ECG machines, heart rate monitors, and blood pressure equipment. If you have questions about the equipment or the measurement of a particular physiological variable, it is best to speak to your professor.

You may also ask about the faculty's research and whether they have printed copies of the articles they have published. Is the faculty's Curriculum Vita on the Internet so you can get access to them? What courses do they teach and to what extent are students involved in the collection of data and so forth?

State or Private School

Another important question you should think about is this: "Should you attend a state college/university or should you attend a private academic institution?" Either can provide a quality education. However, it is important to point out that in recent years, the private schools have been more active as "change makers" in exercise physiology more so than the state institutions. This may be due to the lack of an established history at these institutions, thus change is easier and usually faster.

Tuition is higher at a private school. But, one advantage to paying more at a private college is the increased likelihood of smaller classes, newer courses, and increased hands-on lab time with more personal one-on-one teaching. And, frankly, it is not wrong to ask the

> Private schools have more flexibility and quicker turn-around response in updating the curriculum than many state schools.

question: "Why apply to a state school when 98% of the schools have academic majors in kinesiology (or human performance or exercise science) and not exercise physiology?" Frankly, this is "the" reason why private schools and smaller, less well-known state schools have become leaders in the field.

The application process to both institutions is essentially the same. The good news is that it is just a matter of time when there will be more ASEP accredited institutions. Until then, you should consider applying to schools that have an excellent exercise physiology core of courses. In this way, at graduation, you can sit for the EPC exam and become a board certified exercise physiologist. Do not let exercise physiologists who do not support the certification dissuade you from becoming an EPC. This latter point is simply a statement of fact since exercise physiology is not immune to the political, economic, and social influences, as is true with most other healthcare professions.

Part Two

Exercise Physiology

Success is a process rather than an event. Students do not always know how or when, but each one wants to stand for something. Being an exercise physiologist is an excellent way to make a difference.

Will yourself to succeed by studying hard, to step out of the ranks of the average, to make your mark. Dare to excel in college, to try new ideas, to take risks in research projects, and to grow as a healthcare professional. Start living exercise physiology today.

Chapter Five

What is Exercise Physiology?

Future healthcare trends in exercise physiology are promising.

For the past several decades, exercise physiology has been identified as an academic discipline with its primary mission being research. While research is still very important, the emphasis now is on the application of the exercise physiology body of knowledge to healthcare issues and concerns. The leaders of the ASEP organization are responsible for the new perspective on exercise physiology.

. Now, with greater emphasis on the prevention of disease, health promotion, and quality of life in addition to maximizing fitness and sports training, the value placed on the integrated body of knowledge that defines exercise physiology has increased tremendously. All of this clearly means more and better career opportunities for exercise physiology students.

It is an exciting time to be entering the field. More than ever before, with the 21st century healthcare image of exercise physiology, the public is getting the message: "Exercise physiologists are competent professionals with excellent decision-making and problem-solving skills." The exercise physiologist is not by title a personal trainer or fitness professional, but the exercise physiologist would make a great personal, professional consultant on fitness matters.

- **How does the public view exercise physiology?**
- **How do exercise physiologists define what they do?**

These are important questions. The answers are somewhat less definite than most in the field would like to think. Popular textbooks still define exercise physiology as "the study of acute and chronic adaptations to exercise." The definition is consistent with the historical interest in research. As such, it is a very narrow view of exercise physiology. The problem with the definition is that it defines a discipline not a profession. Hence, since the founding of the *American Society of Exercise Physiologists* in 1997, it was important to update the definition.

Of course, there is the ASEP definition [1] that is consistent with exercise physiology as a healthcare profession. The ASEP leadership is convinced that the contemporary changes in education, especially with regard to combining quality with innovation, along with the technological advances to deliver better healthcare have revolutionized exercise physiology.

The Kinesiology Influence

Academic exercise physiologists face the ultimate paradox. Keep everything as it has been or change everything. It is no longer enough to change just a few things. Success requires engaging a completely new paradigm (i.e., a new mind-set). That is exactly what the ASEP leadership has done. Their shift in thinking has created a new way of thinking about exercise physiology.

But, first, a little history is important to clarify a few things about exercise physiology. To begin with, the "physiology of exercise" course was one of four (kinesiology, sports biomechanics, and sports nutrition) core courses required in the physical education major. Since physical education was not believed to merit serious educational value (which of course was not true), many leaders within . physical education decided to call it by another name. Unfortunately, they did not identify just one name. Today, leading physical education programs go by dozens of different names (or titles).

Kinesiology is a term that was proposed by the *American Academy of Kinesiology and Physical Education* (AAKPE) as an alternative title to the physical education title [2]. The official stamp of approval was in 1989 when the Academy encouraged departments and/or divisions to adopt the term kinesiology. Mixed feelings resulted in the use of numerous titles, such as exercise science or human performance. Reaction to the earlier proposal and the lack of guidelines resulted in 40 or more different department titles with just as many different academic degree titles.

> The quandary faced by physical educators compares with the plethora of titles used to describe exercise physiology.

Titles like exercise specialist, bioenergetics, and sports sciences are equally confusing to students and the public. Of course, they are professionally inappropriate and philosophically misleading. The effort to stabilize physical education failed to take into consideration the need for an autonomous existence of exercise physiology. As a result, students often end up confused as to where physical education ends and exercise physiology starts.

The ASEP Definitions

Driven by the re-conceptualization of exercise physiology as a healthcare profession, the ASEP leaders adopted the following definition:

> The **ASEP Exercise Physiologist** is a person who has an academic degree in exercise physiology, or who is certified by ASEP to practice exercise physiology [via the Exercise Physiologist Certified exam (EPC)], or who has a doctorate degree with an academic degree or emphasis in exercise physiology from an accredited college or university.

> The **profession of Exercise Physiology** is the identification of physiological mechanisms underlying physical activity, the comprehensive delivery of treatment services concerned with the analysis, improvement, and maintenance of health and fitness, rehabilitation of heart disease and other chronic diseases and/or disabilities, and the professional guidance and counsel of athletes and others interested in athletics, sports training, and human adaptability to acute and chronic exercise.

Note that ASEP certification is the link to the professional title.

> **The ASEP definitions are not just new, but practical and absolutely imperative.**

Also, of considerable importance is the decision that the ASEP certification holds the exercise physiologist accountable to the ASEP Code of Ethics [3] and the ASEP Standards of Practice. In this way, the exercise physiologist is viewed as a credible professional who is held accountable for what he or she does with clients.

The definitions are awesome for two reasons. First, they reinforce the idea that "physiology" is critical to all exercise physiologists, especially those interested in athletics. Second, they drive home that the exercise physiologist's knowledge is delivered as "treatment services."

Brief History of Exercise Physiology

Some say that the history of exercise physiology goes back to Europe with research on muscular exercise. A.V. Hill of Britain introduced the term "maximal oxygen intake" (VO_2 max) in 1924. The quest to understand the physiology of athletics and human performance goes back to then and beyond and continues even today with the work of David B. Dill of the Harvard Fatigue Laboratory. Much of Dill's work formed the basis of the development of exercise physiology in the United States.

By the 1950s and 1960s, physical educators with an interest in the development and maintenance of physical training programs to improve health-related adult fitness and athletics helped to lead the way toward new fitness

> **The concept of an "exercise prescription" surfaced after detailed scientific work in exercise physiology.**

programs in schools. Their research helped to develop many adult fitness programs, which were used as an early template for the testing and rehabilitation of patients with coronary heart disease.

With the increased interest in the benefits of regular exercise, more universities expanded the physical education departments to include an academic

38

concentration in exercise science. A few departments offered a concentration (or emphasis) in exercise physiology. The expansion of both was accompanied by an increase in research laboratories in which the data from the physiological studies were published in research journals in physical education and other established scientific journals. Many of these research articles now represent much of the scientific knowledge that defines the profession of exercise physiology.

Thomas K. Cureton of the University of Illinois directed a very productive laboratory with many research publications on a variety of strength and fitness topics. Much of his work was directed at understanding athletic performance. In fact, sports training research has been at the forefront of the field for decades. Ultimately, the increase in physical education programs with an academic emphasis in either exercise science or exercise physiology resulted in the development of "new" professionals referred to as exercise physiologists.

By comparison to physical educators who were trained to understand scientific principles, exercise physiologists were usually better prepared to conduct research. They also had more access to research laboratories with state-of-the-art metabolic equipment. During the early 1970s through the 1990s, with continued interest in fitness and rehabilitation, the need to present research, to come together as professionals with a common interest in research findings, and the importance of certification to increase credibility of the graduates, the membership of the *American College of Sports Medicine* was significantly increased [4]. Some of the original members were involved in the development of the research journal, *Medicine and Science in Sports and Exercise.* It was the first-ever credible research outlet for exercise physiologists and others interested in sports training and human performance.

The founding of other professional societies includes the *American Association of Cardiovascular and Pulmonary Rehabilitation* [5] and the *American Society of Exercise Physiologists.* The latter professional society was founded in 1997 specifically for exercise physiologists. In additional to other professional documents, ASEP publishes two electronic journals.

39

> **The JEPonline is the first scientific, peer-reviewed "electronic" journal that publishes original exercise physiology research manuscripts and review articles.**

the *Journal of Exercise Physiologyonline* and the *Professionalization of Exercise Physiologyonline.*

As the professional organization of exercise physiologists, ASEP developed the board certification for exercise physiologists and the first accreditation guidelines along with the first-ever Code of Ethics. The growth and development of exercise physiology is directly related to the founding of ASEP, graduates from the accredited institutions, the public's recognition of certified exercise physiologists, and the number and quality of research and professional publications.

The type of research carried out by exercise physiologists is diverse. From healthcare to athletics, there are many opportunities to do original research. The following list represents a random selection from the JEPonline journal [6]:

1. Central and peripheral circulatory responses during four different recovery positions immediately following submaximal exercise
2. Effect of diet and exercise on quality of life and fitness parameters among obese individuals
3. Carbohydrate supplementation fails to improve the sprint performance of female cyclists
4. Noninvasive characterization of the blood pressure response to the double-leg press exercise
5. The effect of training while breathing oxygen-enriched air on time-to-exhaustion and aerobic capacity
6. Performance of altitude acclimatized and non-acclimatized professional football (soccer) players at 3,600 m
7. Incidence of the oxygen plateau at VO_2max during exercise testing to volitional fatigue

8. The oxygen cost of walking

9. Physical fitness outcomes in a pulmonary rehabilitation program utilizing symptom limited interval training and resistance training

10. Physiology of yoga and different meditation practices

11. Detecting the onset of added cardiovascular strain during combined arm and leg exercise

12. The surprising history of the "HRmax = 220-age" equation

13. The effects of respiratory muscle training on VO_2 max, the ventilatory threshold and pulmonary function

14. Caloric cost of martial arts training in novice participants

15. Acute hypoxia alters lactate threshold in chronic altitude residents

---

The first issue of the PEPonline journal was published in 1998.

PEPonline was created to promote professionalism and professional development among exercise physiologists. The ability to describe, research, and publish articles about professionalism, ethics, and work-related job opportunities, issues, and concerns within the profession and in the public sector has had a positive impact on exercise physiology. The following list is a sample of the articles published in PEPonline [7]:

1. Exercise physiology: new professional challenges

2. Rising to the level of "profession"

3. Defining the exercise physiologist

4. The exercise physiologist as an entrepreneur

5. Accreditation

6. Leadership issues in exercise physiology

7. The passionate pursuit of professionalism: a critical analysis

8. Making a professional commitment

9. Meeting the standards of a profession

10. What's in a title?

11. Undergraduate programs in exercise science / exercise physiology: issues and concerns

12. Taking responsibility for professionalism

13. Exercise physiology quackery and consumer fraud

14. Analysis and comparison of colleges and universities with degree titles of exercise physiology or related titles

15. Exercise as medication: an exercise physiologist's view

16. Legal dimensions of exercise physiology practice

17. Helping students understand the need for professionalism

The Center for Exercise Physiology-online, the sister organization [8] to ASEP, publishes the *Journal of Professional Exercise Physiology* (JPEP). It is a free electronic journal dedicated to the professional issues of exercise physiology. The following topics represent the types of articles JPEP publishes [9]:

1. Professionalization of exercise physiology: images, issues, and trends

2. Fundamentals of exercise physiology professionalism

3. The exercise physiology job search: a guide

4. Sports, its purpose, and dietary supplements

5. The culture of exercise physiology

6. We can change our future

7. Medical ethics in exercise physiology

8. Thankfulness

ASEP exercise physiologists have found ways to embrace the 21st century [10]. To do so required them to look through a completely different lens. This new world of exercise physiology is characterized by professional development and accountability. There is no going back.

Chapter Six

What are the Career Opportunities?

The accreditation of exercise physiology programs is producing credible career options in the public sector.

When thinking of any healthcare profession, it is important to keep in mind the old adage: "Nothing is certain except change." Changes come in many forms. Some changes are the result of choices we make. Some are part of the normal progression of how people think. This

> **Managing change is an integral part of what the ASEP leaders are doing.**

is the case with the changes in exercise physiology. Because of our choices in recent years, we are no longer a discipline but rather a profession. Increasingly, students are getting better jobs with more responsibility, autonomy, and pay. They are saying goodbye to the gym jobs and the jobs without medical benefits. Many students believe in the exciting career possibilities of the future. They have a positive outlook and are eager to get started.

ASEP leaders have been proactive in changing exercise physiology. In today's business of healthcare, the ASEP accreditation, board certification, and

> **Thinking new helps to restore faith in leaders.**

standards of practice are huge transformations of exercise physiology. Although the impact of each is dramatic, when viewed collectively, they represent a major makeover of exercise physiology. ASEP leaders are open-minded about "exercise" and career opportunities. They believe that yesterday's thinking is inadequate to achieve success in the 21st century and that yesterday's practices neglected the students primary concern (i.e., professional credibility).

Professional innovation and philosophic changes emerged with the founding of the ASEP organization. Those who understood its importance were willing to provide the resources necessary to ensure its success. Part of this new rationale is targeting the powerful belief that "exercise is better than medicine." While exercise physiologists have always placed an emphasis on prevention, they did not do it from the healthcare-professional perspective.

New ethical and legal issues have arisen because it is essential that healthcare professionals are credible [1]. Fortunately, the restructuring of exercise physiology around new ASEP thinking is the first significant step for increased credibility. The first requirement, among many, was to develop a credible Board of Certification for exercise physiologists. EPCs are recognized as professionals who are registered with *The Center for Exercise Physiology-online.*

With professional credentials, including the ASEP designated academic course work, internship hours, and hands-on laboratory experiences, the public sector can rest assured that the conduct and client interaction of exercise physiologists are consistent with other healthcare professionals. Certified [2] exercise physiologists are committed to the best health and fitness programs in:

1. **Private homes**
2. **Corporate wellness**
3. **Military training centers**
4. **Cardiac and/or pulmonary rehabilitation programs**
5. **University fitness centers**
6. **Industrial settings with clients of all ages**
7. **Retail businesses in the promotion of fitness and athletic products**
8. **Lifestyle risk factor assessments clinics and/or centers**
9. **Research activities**
10. **Obesity and aging rehabilitation programs**

44

Exercise Physiology Researcher

Exercise physiology related careers include working in research laboratories and in medical equipment and pharmaceutical companies. Exercise physiologists in these positions use their extensive knowledge of anatomy, cardiovascular and applied physiology, research design and statistics, laboratory knowledge to evaluate research proposals, collect data and analyze it, and to develop reports and manuscripts.

> **Career opportunity begins with diversity in thinking and academic training. Students should take a variety of courses.**

- Employers include pharmaceutical and medical supply companies, Olympic and sports medicine outlets, and academic and/or clinical rehabilitation programs. Employers look for well-round individuals with good research and laboratory skills, knowledge of statistics and report preparation, including good interpersonal, business, and management training. Salaries often begin at approximately $32,000 for laboratory research to $45,000 (pharmaceuticals) depending on academic preparation and professional experience.

Exercise Physiology Consultant and/or Instructor

Increasingly, not only are exercise physiologists working in healthcare, but they are also working as consultants and instructors. Many of these positions are found in sports and athletics. The exercise physiology curriculum encourages the application of its content in sports consulting, psychological preparedness and training of athletes, personal health and fitness training and counseling, exercise and sports biomechanics, and exercise and sports nutrition.

Health, fitness, and wellness promotion is the cornerstone for employment of exercise physiologists. Issues underlying health, fitness, and wellness are major concerns in the public sector. Exercise physiologists are employed as managers, consultants, directors, and professional trainers throughout the community in health and fitness clubs, YMCA/YWCAs, private businesses, and a variety of other lifestyle oriented community programs.

The academic degree in exercise physiology is the professional credential for professionals who are interested in encouraging clients to take increased responsibility for their own health through informed lifestyle choices. Many jobs in this area may be found within large corporations, fitness, and wellness facilities that contract with individuals for personal and corporate fitness and lifestyle management. Many professionals also work with local public sector correctional agencies, police, and firemen.

Salaries start from about $28,000 (private clubs) to $30,000 per year (corporate fitness and wellness) and even as high as $35,000 to $45,000 per year depending upon academic and professional experience, professional certification, the employer, and the market. Personal trainers, as exercise physiology business entrepreneurs, with excellent academic, interpersonal, and business skills may earn as much as $50,000 to $100,000 per year!

Exercise Physiology Clinician

An employment area that is popular for many exercise physiology students and those in the public sector without the doctorate degree is cardiac rehabilitation. In this environment, exercise physiologists supervise exercise tests and patients in hospitals settings by providing patient education and monitoring of blood pressure and heart rate during exercise.

Exercise physiologists also act as primary Case Managers within a new participant orientation process, which includes producing therapy and physician progress reports on a regular

Exercise physiologists act as Case Managers.

basis. They are responsible for group exercise classes that deal with flexibility training, muscular development and weight lifting techniques. They provide instructions regarding running styles and exercise intensity, along with patient education on coronary artery disease risk factors and, where appropriate, the design and recommendation of a specific exercise prescription and modification.

The exercise physiologist in the hospital setting works with patients who have coronary artery disease. But, given that there are rehabilitation programs for patients with lung disease (including patients with COPD), diabetes, obesity, rheumatoid arthritis, dyslipoproteinemia (elevated cholesterol), cystic fibrosis, hypertension (high blood pressure), low functional capacity, and pregnancy, and given that exercise is central to the patients' rehabilitation, exercise physiologists work closely with physiotherapists, occupational therapists, nurses, and physicians in sports medicine clinics and private sector cardiology suites and rehabilitation centers. Salaries start from $28,000 to $35,000 per year with higher salaries for master-prepared exercise physiologists.

Under the supervision of a medical doctor or cardiovascular nurse, exercise physiologists perform resting and exercise electrocardiographic (ECG) and related examinations of patients in accordance with established graded exercise tests standards and practices. For example, they may:

- Perform electrocardiograph examinations and others as ordered
- Demonstrate knowledge of the principles of growth and development over the life span of the assigned patient population
- Assess and interpret patient age specific data and provides appropriate, age specific treatment
- Provide direct patient care to assigned patient age group(s)
- Set up and check equipment for stress testing and administers exercise test to patients
- Explain graded exercise test procedures to patient, and evaluate the patient's cardiovascular and musculoskeletal condition and response throughout the test
- Record and calculate all ECG parameters and interpret ECG tracings for diagnostic purposes
- Submit ECG tracings to physicians for diagnostic analysis
- Schedule patient appointments
- Obtain patient history, answer questions, and explain procedures

- Prepare documentation as required by the profession and the department, such as evaluation results, individualized treatment plans, progress reports, and other such reports, and
- Maintain records of examination data and other pertinent information on patients.

Exercise Physiology Ergonomist

Exercise physiologists are also involved in analyzing the work environment of employees. They look at the work conditions, tools, workspaces, and specific physical demands of a job.

Exercise physiologists with ergonomic courses and training are especially interested in repetitive conditions of the employee's work to decrease or eliminate musculoskeletal strain and/or overuse injuries. As an ergonomist, exercise physiologists may be responsible for designing new workspaces and equipment [3]. They may work as a consultant in industries that require repetitive movements. Salaries range from about $28,000 to $38,000 per year to $75,000 or more for senior positions.

> **The objective is to improve employee health and productivity.**

Exercise Physiology Military Professional

The military (Air Force and Army) hires exercise physiologists as Installation Program Fitness Managers to oversee the military policies and facilities for fitness testing and training [4]. They are expected to demonstrate high individual responsibility and application of exercise physiology to testing, prescription, and training.

Exercise Physiology Coach/Trainer

Driven by participants who want more information about skill preparation and athletic competition, exercise physiologists are hired as personal coaches and trainers. As strength coaches, directors, and managers of state and national athletic teams, exercise physiologists apply their specialized body of knowledge to sports development and training. Fortunately, as critical thinkers, with the ability to make good judgments and decisions about sports participation and athletic competition, they are an excellent fit. Salaries range in the $25,000 to $35,000 per year getting started.

Exercise Physiology Wellness Coach

Wellness Coaches USA [5] is frequently looking to fill full-time exercise physiology positions throughout the United States. Jobs are 40 hours per week. Candidates are expected to have the bachelor's degree with a minimum of 2 to 3 years experience in the field. Knowledge of Microsoft office and data entry is also important along with managerial experience.

The Wellness Coach must be outgoing, personable, able to work independently, and possess excellent interpersonal and organization skills. Background in athletic training, injury prevention, ergonomics, wellness, conditioning, health promotion, and public speaking is helpful. Wellness Coaches represents an excellent opportunity to become a part of one of the fastest growing health promotion and injury prevention

> **The Wellness Coach is expected to work one-on-one with the staff, supervisors, and management to assist them in the prevention of workplace and non-workplace injuries and illness.**

companies in America. A position with the company usually allows the exercise physiologist to use personal skills in a challenging, exciting and rewarding work setting, while offering rapid career growth opportunities.

The mission of Wellness Coaches is to help their clients contain the cost of workplace injury and health benefits, and enhance the quality of life of the employees. They are a provider of pro-active, pre-injury, health, and wellness services. Their programs are directed toward the human aspect of injury prevention and health promotion, emphasizing motivation to improve behaviors, education, training, and pre-injury intervention.

Salary ranges up to $50,000, depending on experience and qualifications, plus full benefits (e.g., Laptop, 3 Weeks Paid Time Off, Cell Phone and Internet Allowances, Continuing Education Re-Imbursement, 401k, Health, Dental, and Life).

Wellness Program Coordinator

Healthcare facilities look for qualified exercise physiologists to develop and administer Wellness Programs. The Wellness Program Coordinator works with the employer to develop, implement, communicate and monitor a wellness program specifically designed for their associates.

The objective is to improve the health and wellness of the associates by targeting a variety of issues (e.g., diet, nutrition, obesity, exercise, health, diabetes, smoking, and low back pain). The Coordinator assists in the development of the communication and branding strategy for the program and markets the program effectively throughout the employee population. In addition, exercise physiologists conduct educational seminars and wellness events for the employees in retail and analyze group health plan data in an effort to develop customized wellness programs.

Chapter Seven

Attributes, Skills, and Profiles of Exercise Physiologists

The grassroots of applying the scientific body of knowledge of exercise physiology exist outside of the academic setting.

Employers expect students who have recently graduated with an exercise physiology degree to posses the analytical and hands-on skills to do the job. Of course not all students are equally qualified, and some are clearly more qualified than others. Employers want to hire the best graduate, not the second best. The primary method of identifying the best candidate among the pool of candidates is the "interview." This is why it is important to be prepared when the opportunity arises to interview for a specific job. Employers will evaluate personal attributes in addition to academic preparation and technical skills. They will assess the candidate's ability to communicate though question and answer periods and how the candidate interacts with others during the interview process. They know that social skills are increasingly important to being an effective employee. Should they hire the candidate, they want to be confident that he/she represents the company, business, or institution in a

> **Employers will be on the lookout for how well you write, speak, and interact with others during the interview.**

professional and credible manner. They want to be comfortable with the candidate's ability to mentor other employees, make a sound and accurate presentation, or participate as a credible member of a team either when working with other employees in the company or when working with members of the public.

Students should have as many of these skills at graduation as possible. Hence, if you are academically well prepared, if you possess the right social and communicative skills, and if you understand how to problem-solve and work through new ideas, you are likely to earn high marks during the interview. But, just in case, you might want to study the following questions for answers specific to your skills, abilities, and career expectations:

- Are you self-reliant?
- Do you accept responsibility for your work?
- Are you alert or imaginative?
- Are you an ethical exercise physiologist?
- Can you work with a team?
- Are you a loner?
- Are persistent in your work?
- Where do you get your ideas?
- Are you attentive to details?
- What is your usual communication skill with co-workers?
- How do you keep up with new ideas and trends?
- Are you a good writer?
- Can you write scientifically?
- How would you go about solving a problem?
- What are your Internet skills?
- Do you set personal and/or professional goals?
- What are your career goals?
- Are you a quick learner?
- Do you have the ability to multi-task, or manage several tasks at once?
- Are you detailed-oriented with manual dexterity?
- Do you have good people skills?
- Are you a big-picture thinker?
- How do you handle emotional stress?

Choosing the Right College

Making the right decision about career opportunities is linked to choosing the right college or university to attend [1]. Will the courses that define the academic major move you in the direction that you want to go? Are the professors interested in teaching you or is it apparent that they are more interested in their research? Answers to these questions early on rather than later will benefit you in reaching your goals.

Explore the academic options. Ask your parents, friends, counselors, teachers, and others about the decision to be an

> Choosing the right college and academic major requires careful planning [2].

exercise physiologist? Remember: It is always a good idea to speak with an exercise physiologist in your area of interest. Among other questions, ask the questions: "How do exercise physiologists find jobs, and what is the salary range for a person with an exercise science degree versus the exercise physiology degree?" Understandably, salaries vary by state, geographical region, and education. On average, wages increase with extra years of education. With more education, there are better benefits, better working conditions, and increased job security.

The following content represents a brief collection of comments from exercise physiologists who graduated from The College of St. Scholastica in Duluth, MN [3]. They have agreed to share their professional experiences following graduation. Please note that their comments are *in first person* to personalize the interaction with you.

Pat

I work for a medically based fitness management company called LifeStyle Management [4]. We have several sites (private and corporate) that manage fitness facility and services. We have about 20 employees with the title, professional trainers. All employees have degrees in related fields, but I am the only EPC. There are 10 massage therapists, 10 group exercise instructors, and there are 6 managers, including myself. The managers run the show. Each site varies in size, having between 2 and 15 staff members. Presently, I do all the marketing and program development for the company.

My recent projects include an overhaul of our business website [http://www.lifestylemanagement.net] and development of a "Virtual Training" program. The latter is a personalized exercise DVD for clients with challenging schedules. I also manage our testing office, which I use as a central testing office for several of our sites. This is necessary because we have one metabolic cart. I use this office for testing and training cardiac referrals from our medical director, who is affiliated with the Minneapolis Heart Institute.

The exercise physiology degree from The College of St. Scholastica provided me an excellent knowledge base and critical thinking skills to become an effective communicator with clients. The ability to educate and facilitate the client's understanding of their body and how it responds to exercise is important. Also, the technical skills that I learned in the exercise prescriptions courses and the ability to have a confident, calm "bed-side" manner have allowed me to be an effective tester, trainer,

> **Most importantly, I learned in college how to think, not what to think.**

educator, and program developer. Lastly, if you are going to be successful as an exercise physiologist, you must be a straight thinker. So, when choosing a college, locate one where the professors teach you how to think and not just what to think.

Jody

I have two academic degrees in exercise physiology from St. Scholastica. My wife and family live in Duluth, MN. So, locating a job in clinical exercise physiology at one of the local hospitals was always one of my goals. Just prior to graduation, I mailed a dozen resumes to potential employers.

> **I suppose you can say my tenacity paid off. I am very grateful.**

Eventually, I was hired in Virginia, MN to help start a cardiac rehabilitation program. Aside from the 2-hour daily commute, it was a great job. Working with cardiac patients proved to be the experience I needed. About two years later, a Cardiac Rehabilitation Specialist position opened at St. Mary's Hospital in Duluth, MN. I was hired to work with cardiac patients.

Working in the hospital has been rewarding and challenging. Everyday I recognize the need to keep up with new ideas and research in the field. It is always good to see a smile on the face of a patient who did not know that it was possible to do more work without chest pain. Rehabilitation is just that, however. Although the patient's ability to do more exercise is improved, the physiological changes are for the most part in the muscles and not at the heart level. Helping patients understand the importance of risk factor assessments and lifestyle modifications are integral to living with heart disease.

I am proud to be an exercise physiologist. I think you will be too if you enjoy working with people and helping them to live healthier lives. If I had to leave you with four recommendations, they would be: (1) choose carefully the college or university you attend to become an exercise physiologist; (2) work at believing in yourself and your ability to grow as a critical thinker; (3) never give up when searching for the "right" job; and (4) always stay passionate about your goals in life.

Mitch

I am a Clinical Research Associate for Guidant Corporation [5], which is located in the Twin Cities of Minnesota. I was hired with an undergraduate degree in exercise physiology. Later, while continuing to work at Guidant, I completed the master's degree in exercise physiology from The College of St. Scholastica. Working at Guidant and driving back and forth from Duluth and the Twin Cities (a three-hour drive each way) was a

> **My primary work is in the medical device field.**

bit of a challenge. But, it was worth it. The master's degree increased my salary and improved my chances of moving up in the company.

The medical device field is a relatively new area of work for exercise physiologists with a strong background in research and scientific thinking. Graduates who have had significant hands-on laboratory experiences are expected to do well in the research-oriented company. As an exercise physiologist, my relationship with other researchers, medical doctors, management teams, and those who market the products is good. Much of the interaction that goes on among different professionals must be learned on the job. This is true of other things as well. For example, my interest in the development of the "dual-paced" implantable pacemaker developed while working at Guidant. Pacemakers are complicated, but the use of exercise physiology concepts is woven into the overall analysis and evaluation of the product.

The pay scale for exercise physiologists in the medical device companies is higher than in most cardiac or clinical settings. However, it is important to thoroughly understand the benefits and limitations to the business side of marketing medical-device products. Very long hours and deadlines for product analysis are common in the industry. There also appears to be considerable opportunity for exercise physiologists in the sales department of the company, which may be more lucrative since it is based on commissions.

Sean

After graduating with the master's degree in exercise physiology from The College of St. Scholastica (along with the ASEP certification, the EPC), I got a job at Arete HealthFit [6] in Minnesota. As a professional fitness trainer, I enjoyed working with the clients. It was especially rewarding helping them to achieve their

> **I work for the Medical Graphics company in St. Paul, MN.**

personal fitness goals. However, I must admit that the long hours did not suit my personal lifestyle and professional goals.

I resigned from my position at Arete and applied for an exercise physiology position at Medical Graphics in St. Paul, MN. The company builds metabolic analyzers (like the CardiO2) and other physiological equipment to assess the cardiovascular function of subjects. My primary responsibility is in assisting the customer's use of the metabolic cart and different types of oxygen analyzers in hospital, rehabilitation, and research settings. The work requires troubleshooting the metabolic cart when parts and software fail to operate correctly. Answering questions about the analysis of oxygen consumption along with other related physiological variables comes with the job. I enjoy the work. The money is very good, too.

Nathan

I graduated from St. Scholastica. I have a master's degree in exercise physiology. Following graduation, I was hired at LifeTime Fitness [7] in the Twin Cities, MN. After a brief period, I decided to offer a science-based assessment and testing program to clients. Given its success, and after speaking with the owner of Arete HealthFit (located in Edina, MN), we both agreed that the "assessment and testing program" would do well in Arete. The business has grown from two employees to five with two locations, and it is very likely that it will expand to additional sites.

I believe students should be sponges while in school. They should place themselves in uncomfortable positions and take risks. Doing so will help them deal with the multi-faceted aspects of small businesses that design mailers, brochures, budgets, and develop market plans. If you are the adventurous type, who wants your own business, and you have the work ethic to put in long and hard hours to build an integrated business for personal fitness, weight management, and athletic enhancement, the business of healthcare is wide open and an excellent choice.

Chad

I have a graduate degree in exercise physiology from St. Scholastica. When I graduated, I got a job at Cardiovascular Consultants [8] in Robbinsdale, MN. I want to mention a few things about the importance of a graduate education, especially courses in ECG and stress test protocols. I believe it is important to emphasize the clinical exercise physiology and cardiovascular physiology courses. Both were critical in helping me understand clinical assessments and rehabilitation of patients.

> **Most of my work involves the testing of heart patients and developing individual exercise prescriptions.**

The ECG work and graded exercise testing that I do is for the cardiologists who own the medical practice. They have an excellent working relationship with the exercise physiologists in the practice.

For students interested in working in a medical facility like Cardiovascular Consultants, it is important that they do an internship in cardiac rehabilitation. Get to know the employers. Make as many personal and professional contacts as you can. Networking is important.

Ryan

I have a master's degree in exercise physiology from St. Scholastica. I work at White Bear Racquet and Swim (located in White Bear Lake, MN). Most of my workday is spent as a personal fitness trainer [9]. In addition to my responsibilities for individual clients, I am responsible for musculoskeletal and cardiovascular exercise assessments. I am also responsible for working with clients with diverse physical (and emotional) needs. Exercise physiologists are academically prepared to address many of the healthcare problems clients of all age deal with.

As an employee in the health club industry, I have completed six certifications through several different organizations. I am not an EPC, although I would like to be. I realize and fully understand the benefits of being a board certified exercise physiologist. I believe it is important to gaining the respect of the public sector and other healthcare professionals.

Erin

Following graduation from St. Scholastica with a master's degree in exercise physiology, I was hired by Arete HealthFit. It is a fitness company with two personal training centers in the Twin Cities metro area. At Arete, clients complete a comprehensive fitness evaluation, including measurement of the body composition (via the Bod Pod), resting metabolism, and cardiovascular capacity (via a metabolic analyzer) and receive a personalized fitness program. While at Arete, I worked with clients to help them lose weight, recover from disease, and musculoskeletal injuries. I also worked with athletes and young children. After three years of working at Arete, I decided to go back to school. After completing a master's degree in management, I was interviewed and hired as a Program Director of a rather large company in the Twin Cities, MN.

Shane

For several years, I worked for the United States Air Force as a Program Fitness Manager on three different bases. It was a good job, and the pay was not bad either. But, being from Minnesota, I wanted to raise my family there. So, when I found out about a job at the Community Memorial Homes in Osakis, I applied for it and was hired as the Director of the Exercise Physiology Department. I also started my own company, PhysioLogic Human Performance Systems, which is a consulting company that focuses on the wellness program development.

The undergraduate and graduate degrees from St. Scholastica prepared me with the knowledge I needed to succeed. Beyond the courses, the individualized attention and mentorship from the St. Scholastica professors helped me build the

> **Choosing the right academic institution is absolutely imperative.**

59

confidence to make my dreams come true. I do not think I would have the same aptitude, drive, and passion if I had attended an exercise science program.

Jocee

I am the Fitness Coordinator for the Rehab Institute of Chicago Center for Health and Fitness.

The Rehabilitation Institute of Chicago [10] has been the number one rehab hospital in the United States for the past fifteen consecutive years. The Health and Fitness Center is a 4,000 square foot facility specifically created for people with physical disabilities, spinal cord injuries, multiple sclerosis, cerebral palsy, amputees, and stroke. The purpose of the Center is to help individuals develop, maintain, and improve their physical well being.

My duties at the Institute consist of managing the staff, interns, and fitness center, evaluating patients, designing exercise prescriptions, teaching educational sessions to staff, interns, patients, doctors, and therapists, teaching Arthritis and Parkinson's aerobic classes, developing at home exercise videos for persons with physical disabilities through the National Center on Physical Activity and Disability (NCPAD), being a lead investigator in two grant studies, along with several other miscellaneous duties.

The master's degree in exercise physiology from St. Scholastica has allowed me to give my patients the very best possible analysis, treatment delivery, rehabilitation, and professional guidance. There are only a few accredited colleges with an academic degree in exercise physiology. This is an important reason I attended the College in Duluth, MN. Other reasons include the list of academic courses, the faculty, and the laboratory opportunities.

Chris

In 2003, I was offered an internship and worked for the United States Olympic Committee at the Olympic Training Center in Lake Placid, New York. I trained athletes from winter and summer sports. In addition to Olympic athletes, I had the opportunity to train athletes from the NHL, NFL, NFL-Europe, and MLB, and serve as a lecturer/strength coach for USA Hockey.

> I am a strength and conditioning coach in Duluth, MN.

Just recently, I started a business called Impact Sports Training. It is dedicated to enhancing the performance of athletes. Also, I am currently working with hundreds of local high school and collegiate athletes, as well as the UW-Superior Men and Women Hockey Teams.

Prior to returning to Duluth, I served for two years as the Director of Strength and Conditioning at PerformanceONE Athletic Development in Columbus, Ohio, as well as the Head Strength and Conditioning Coach for the Columbus Destroyers of the Arena Football League.

I am certified by the *National Strength and Conditioning Association* [11] as a Certified Strength and Conditioning Specialist (CSCS), certified by the *American Society of Exercise Physiologists* as a Board Certified Exercise Physiologist (EPC), and certified by *USA Weightlifting* [12] as a Club Coach (USAW).

The master's degree in exercise physiology from St. Scholastica [13] has certainly helped to advance my career as an exercise physiologist. I learned more in the first semester than I did in the four years I spent getting the undergraduate degree in exercise science. I knew that I did not want to spend my career in a clinical setting, so I took my education in a different direction. What it did was to open a lot of doors for me. I got to know as many people as I could in the field, got as much experience as I could regardless of the pay, and made things happen.

It was not long after graduating that I was offered a position as a Director of a large facility. I was offered the job mostly because of the people I knew in the field. Networking is important. It can create career opportunities. One piece of advice for those who are close to choosing the college to attend, do not expect people to offer you a job just because you have a degree. You need to work for it, and it might take a while. Just like a tool, a degree is worthless unless you use it.

Sarah

I work in Tampa, FL at St. Joseph's Hospital in Cardiopulmonary Rehabilitation [14]. I work full time as an exercise physiologist and a case manager for about 30 cardiac patients. On Monday, Wednesday, and Friday, I monitor up to 8 patients at a time on 3-lead heart monitors. The ECG monitor helps me to be certain that the patients are exercising safely. Exercise physiologist must know how to prescribe exercise using different heart rate intensity methods. It is also a very effective way to be sure that the patients reach their goals in rehabilitation.

Heart patients in the maintenance program are responsible for their own safety. By this, I

> **Exercise physiologists take the patient's systolic blood pressure before, during, and after exercise.**

mean that they must monitor their own exercise intensity (i.e., heart rate) and blood pressure. Exercise physiologists are present, but their role is primarily to deal with concerns about the patient's vital signs should a patient not feel well. I also oversee a 12-lead ECG analysis during graded exercise testing and teach patient education that addresses primarily information about lipids, risk factors for heart disease, stress management, and exercise precautions.

On Tuesday and Thursday, I work in Pulmonary Rehabilitation. My job is to ensure that the patient's oxygen levels are good during each exercise mode. Of course, with most hospital jobs, the paperwork is tremendous. My department is extremely organized. Each paper has its own designated location, and each requires signatures. It is still a lot of work keeping up with everything.

Having the master's degree has allowed me to relate well to patients. It has also helped me to be confident when dealing directly with the patients. I can educate them efficiently and effectively with the education that I got at the graduate level. There is no way I would have this position in the hospital without the exercise physiology degree. Having the degree allows me to have more choices when it comes to other career opportunities.

Kevin

As a master-prepared exercise physiologist, I am an instructor in the Exercise Science Program at Winston-Salem State University in Winston-Salem, NC. I am

> **I teach functional anatomy, kinesiology, biomechanics, and sports nutrition.**

responsible for health promotion in cardiac rehabilitation as well as the application of physiological training principles to cardiac rehabilitation, adult fitness clients, and athletes [15].

The exercise physiology master's degree from St. Scholastica helped me to reach my goal of teaching exercise physiology at the college level. I feel that I have a strong scientific background in the field. While I plan to continue teaching at the University, I believe it is important to get the doctorate degree. If everything works out just right, I should have the degree in 4 to 5 years.

Danita

After completing the master's degree in exercise physiology at St. Scholastica, I looked at several job possibilities. I decided to be a consultant with an occupational wellness company in Eau Claire, Wisconsin. I enjoy the work. I do group presentations and one-on-one interventions with high-risk employees for cardio-pulmonary disease, obesity, and diabetes. I work in the Duluth area and central Minnesota. I may also start consulting in the Twin Cities Metro area.

I was hired because I am a Registered Dietitian (RD), but the graduate degree increased my hourly contract rate by $10 to $15 per hour over someone without the degree. Also, when it was discovered that my master's degree was in exercise physiology, I was asked to participate in planning exercise challenges. Since most of the high risk employees are at least 35 years old, I am able to work with joint issues, chronic pain, neuropathy related to diabetes or other issues. I

63

can also develop exercise prescriptions for individuals with coronary artery disease.

Joe

Upon completing the master's degree in exercise physiology from The College of St. Scholastica, I moved to Minneapolis to work on the PhD degree at the University of Minnesota [16]. Presently, my research is focused on bone, muscle, and tendon and how these tissues are affected by various loading modalities as well as certain disease states.

While in doctorate school, I traveled to Manchester, England to learn some of the novel and cutting-edge techniques used by a specialized group of professionals to non-invasively assess the mechanical and structural properties of bone and tendon via MRI, ultrasound, and computed tomography. My colleagues and I will attempt to use unique models like ACL reconstruction and stroke to assess the influence of various degrees of unloading magnitude and duration on the musculoskeletal, vascular, and metabolic systems.

Also, I have had the opportunity to teach courses at the University, assist the strength and conditioning coach on a volunteer basis, and co-chair the University

> **Aside from my work at the University, I have my own column in the National Strength and Conditioning Association's *Performance Training Journal.***

of Minnesota Sports Biomechanics Special Interest Group. As a column writer for NSCA, I have written articles about athletics and strength training. This experience has allowed me to serve as a reviewer for journal articles, too.

Jake

After graduating with the master's degree in exercise physiology from The College of St. Scholastica, I joined the Wolfe-Harris Center for Clinical Studies [17]. My primary position is to serve as an Exercise Therapist/Research Assistant for several federally funded randomized clinical trials. My primary responsibilities include performing the initial eligibility screen and the informed consents with potential participants. I also provide supervision and guidance to patients in supervised rehabilitative exercise and home exercise programs. The pay is good, and I have medical benefits.

Erin

At the time I entered the exercise physiology program at St. Scholastica, I knew that I wanted to teach at the college level. Almost upon the completion of my thesis for the master's degree, I applied for a part-time position to teach the laboratory sections of the Human Anatomy and Physiology course in the Biology Department at the University of Wisconsin-Eau Claire. This is my fourth year of teaching at the University.

The part-time position works very well for me. I am married with a daughter, and I am pregnant with my second baby. Other perks of the position are that I receive full medical benefits at only 50% contract. Additionally, I have time for vacation and family. Do not get me wrong, teaching is and can be a burn-out job, and it takes a lot of preparation time to be ready for classes. I enjoy the students, and I enjoy learning.

St. Scholastica and, more specifically, the exercise physiology program enabled me to do what I enjoy doing. I am very grateful for the experience. Further, I have considered going for the doctorate in exercise physiology at St. Scholastica if a program becomes established there. My experiences with the professors were above and beyond what I had expected.

Todd

Exercise Physiology has been good to me through the years. After finishing an internship at the Rehabilitation Institute of Chicago, I worked at Unity/Mercy hospital in the cardiac rehabilitation department. This led me to an opportunity just outside of New Orleans as the Director of Community and Corporate Health

Exercise Programs at St. Charles Parish Hospital. They hired me to start the programs from the ground up. I worked there for just over three years and during that time met my wife. That is what brought me to Wisconsin where I went back to school to earn a nursing degree. I am currently a licensed nurse working at a small rural hospital in Wisconsin.

Ann

After completing the undergraduate degree in exercise physiology at St. Scholastica, I started working as a Physiology Lab Instructor for in the Biology Department at St. Scholastica. Many of the laboratory exercises deal with physiological processes that I studied while a student in the exercise physiology major (i.e.,

> **I have been accepted as a graduate student at George Washington University to complete a Master's degree in Public Health (MPH).**

cardiac function, ECG, muscle contraction, respiratory function, blood pressure, metabolism, and anatomy). With my academic background, I was well prepared to answer questions and relate the concepts covered in class. I should also add that the exercise physiology program helped me to develop greater concern for promoting public health through education and healthcare policy. That is why I have decided to pursue a master's degree in public health.

Jonathan

I am working as an exercise physiologist at St. Mary's Health Center in St. Louis, MO. I work with cardiac patients in Phases II and III on site at the hospital. At the present time, I am the only exercise physiologist working at St. Mary's. Lately, I have thought a lot about applying to Physician Assistant schools. If I do so, my patient care experience will greatly increase my chances of being accepted into the programs.

Tim

I work for the PRACS Institute. It is the largest privately owned pharmaceutical research facility in North America. We do research studies for pharmaceutical companies. My responsibility is to make sure these studies are completed correctly, successfully, and with high quality assurance. When completing the master's thesis at St. Scholastica, it was my responsibility to make sure that all testing was done correctly. The experience helped tremendously with my current employment.

Jeremy

Presently, I live on a small ranch in Colorado. I work as a personal trainer at Bally Total Fitness and at a local ski shop. My clients have been (and will continue to be) impressed with my vast knowledge of exercise physiology. I plan to sit for the NSCA-CSCS certification exam. It seems to me that the St. Scholastica exercise physiology degree with the CSCS certification will help me secure a strength coach position with a college or professional basketball team. Also, another route I may choose to take is to train alpine skiers. I would like to eventually start my own business where I would cater to those who come to Colorado for extended periods of time to ski/snowboard. The business would be geared towards altitude acclimation for the clientele.

Chapter Eight

Salaries, Benefits, Perks, and Jobs

The culminating concept in career opportunities is money.

Starting salaries in exercise physiology and other healthcare professions depend on the demand for exercise physiologists. Since "exercise" is an important variable in dealing with risk factors for many different

> **Exercise physiologists must be ASEP board certified.**

diseases, exercise physiology will be an important career option for many students. Exercise is believed to be useful in the prevention, treatment, and/or rehabilitation of numerous diseases.

With the founding of the *American Society of Exercise Physiologists*, there is now a regulatory process associated with the professional title, Exercise Physiologist. As stated in earlier chapters, it is now defined by the EPC exam that certifies the exercise physiologist as a healthcare professional. If a person is not an EPC or if a person does not have a doctorate degree (or academic concentration) in exercise physiology, the person is not an exercise physiologist.

The *National Association of Colleges and Employers* has published a starting salary range for selected areas of study [1]. It is useful for comparison of salaries. The ranges are exactly that, however. They present the earning potential across the board (i.e., the average salary ranges). Depending on the geographic location, type of job (i.e., company or industry), and the responsibilities that associate with a job, the starting salaries will vary. Aside from the salary, there are other important variables that might be important too.

> **Some healthcare professionals are encouraged to relocate with pot sweeteners, like bonuses, relocation expenses, and start-up money.**

From a regional perspective, it is always good to know something about the geographic region, cost-of-living, medical benefits, and perks.

The following list of starting salary ranges is presented for comparative purposes only. One should not get overly excited or depressed from this list.

Accounting	$36,000-$43,500
Business Administration/Management	$30,000-$42,000
Economics/Finance (incl. Banking)	$34,000-$45,000
Hospitality Services Management	$28,000-$34,500
Marketing/Marketing Management	$29,750-$38,500
Elementary Teacher Education	$26,000-$34,500
English Language/Literature	$22,000-$33,000
History	$27,500-$35,000
Political Science/Government	$21,216-$34,000
Psychology	$20,000-$32,000

Exercise physiologists may be employed in diverse settings:

1. In community organizations, they conduct exercise programs for health maintenance, cardiac risk identification, and rehabilitation.

2. In commerce and industry, exercise physiologists provide health and fitness evaluation, exercise prescription, and overall program management in spas, health clubs, or recreation centers.

3. Of course, there are numerous opportunities in the hospital settings whereby they work with other healthcare professionals in providing rehabilitation programs for cardiology departments, respiratory, obesity, and physical therapy centers, and musculoskeletal rehabilitation clinics.

4. Others work in a variety of sports medicine clinics. They work to prevent and rehabilitate athletic injuries as well as to promote the correct sports training principles.

The job outlook is good due to the increased emphasis on prevention of illness and on exercise as a viable method to promote good health. Also, there are many career opportunities for research on aging, rehabilitation of age-related conditions, and the emotional health benefits of exercise. For comparison purposes, the following salary range is presented for the graduate with the bachelor's degree.

Exercise Physiologists	**$28,000 - $35,000**

With the master's degree, the exercise physiologist's salary is usually around $32,000 to $42,000 for 12 months (with an average starting salary of $37,000). Understandably, this salary is with the master's degree. But, it does compare rather well with the following average starting salaries:

Registered nurses	$38,419
Licensed practical nursing	$27,548
Radiology	$35,623
Computer technologies	$34,647
Health information technology	$27,481
Medical lab technician	$33,299
Medical assistant	$23,983

Other factors such as the advanced (doctorate) degree and board certification may also influence pay scales. In general, the doctorate prepared exercise physiologist starts an academic position around $55,000 for 9 months. The top salaries are directly correlated with tenure and years of teaching (including administrative experience) along with a record of publishing scientific papers and books. Most exercise physiologists with the doctorate degree work in educational settings where they teach courses such as exercise physiology, medicine, physiology, and other health related fields (e.g., physical therapy and nutrition) and do research. Others work in hospital settings as program directors of cardiac rehabilitation programs. A good number of these exercise physiologists will also be involved in research studies.

Internet Job Postings

ExerciseCareers.com

There are dozens of Internet companies that post jobs and career opportunities for exercise physiologists. The following is a brief list on the *ExerciseCareers.com/* website [2]:

1. *Job Title:* **Exercise Therapist**

   Company: Fitness for Health, Inc.

   Location: Rockville, MD

   Job Description: Work with children with disabilities in a private fitness facility in Rockville MD. Full-time or part-time positions are available.

   Salary: Competitive.

2. *Job Title:* **Exercise Physiologist**

   Company: G2 Fitness Institute

   Location: Jackson, MS

   Job Description: Outstanding job opportunity

   Salary: Above average salary and benefits.

3. *Job Title:* **Cardiopulmonary Technologist**

   Company: Frontera Strategies

   Location: Houston, TX

   Job Description: Frontera, the leader in cardiopulmonary exercise testing, is seeking talented, energetic candidates to conduct mobile metabolic exercise testing at our physicians' offices. Prior cardiac and stress testing experience is required. Master's degree in exercise physiology or related field is required. Great training and mentoring offered, along with full benefits! Positions open in Houston and Austin. In-state candidates preferred.   Please do not apply if you do not meet the minimum requirements listed above.

Salary: Not mentioned.

4. *Job Title:* **Exercise Physiologist**

   Company: Fitcorp

   Location: Boston, Massachusetts

   Job Description: Fitcorp, Boston's leading provider of fitness and wellness programs is hiring full-time Exercise Physiologists.   Job responsibilities include:

   - Providing fitness orientation, assessments, and follow-up to all members;
   - Preparing individual fitness programs for members and offer program reviews; and
   - Performing timely and effective floor work with members, building relationships and providing assistance as needed.

   Candidates must possess 1 to 2 years experience with fitness assessments and exercise prescription.

   Salary: Fitcorp has an excellent benefits package.

There are other listings for exercise physiologists who want to work in the health and fitness area.   Again, this list was on the *ExerciseCareers.com/* website [http://www.exercisecareers.com/]:

1. *Job Title:* **Exercise Fitness Instructor Specialist**

   Company: Green Mountain at Fox Run

   Location: Ludlow, Vermont

   Job Description: Green Mountain at Fox Run, a nationally-renowned, professionally-directed residential weight and health lifestyle program exclusively for women seeks to fill its lead fitness position.   Candidates

73

must possess· strong interpersonal and communication skills and enjoy working directly with clients. The responsibilities include

- Conducting lectures/workshops;
- Teaching fitness classes including weight training with free weights, machines, resistance bands and balls, aerobics fitness, circuit and interval training;
- Dancing, yoga, tai chi a real plus, but not required; and
- Conducting individual consults, exercise modification and prescription required.

Interest with curriculum development and personal training not necessary, but opportunity to develop exists. Position offers great challenges for the individual seeking a non-traditional setting for using his/her expert fitness and motivational skills along with a team of professionals in psychology, nutrition, metabolism, and stress management. The ability to work enthusiastically and discreetly with both a fit and fitness-compromised population is essential. Position requires high energy, hands-on creative person who enjoys working with people on a day-to-day basis.

Salary: Salary and benefits are competitively based on experience. BS/BA candidates with a bona fide professional certification required. At least 2+ years of field experience with group fitness classes.

2. *Job Title:* **Fitness Specialist**

   Company: FitWell Associates, Inc.

   Location: Washington, District of Columbia

   Job Description: FitWell Associates, Inc. is a fitness management and consulting firm committed to helping clients increase productivity with comprehensive fitness solutions that deliver customer satisfaction. We provide trustworthy on-site fitness center management that is effective, successful and healthy for all clients through our people, our technology, and partnerships. FitWell provides top-notch fitness and wellness services to some of our nation's most significant public and private organizations. We understand how to provide a high level of customer service consistent with the interests and needs of the fitness center members. Job responsibilities include

- Administering fitness evaluations, exercise program orientations, and fitness re-evaluations;
- Providing on-going guidance to members on the proper use of exercise equipment and their exercise programs;
- Developing, supervising, and instructing aerobic exercise and exercise classes;
- Monitoring exercise program satisfaction and progress;
- Planning and implementing a variety of fitness programs (such as physical conditioning, walking, running, strength training, and flexibility);
- Maintaining facility and equipment and keep a daily log of facility and equipment maintenance needs;
- Leading group exercise classes;
- Overseeing membership attendance and evaluation records;
- Designing and implementing incentive and health promotion programs;
- Performing administrative tasks associated with the facility; and
- Supervising student interns.

Qualifications include: (a) experience teaching cardiovascular group exercise classes; (b) BS/BA exercise physiology, health fitness or related field; (c) aerobic certification; (d) current CPR certification; (e) ability to work effectively with a diverse member population; and (f) excellent interpersonal and organizational skills.

Salary: Not mentioned.

3. *Job Title:* **Fitness Specialist**

   Company: The Industrial Athlete

   Location: Clinton Township, Michigan

   Job Description: Full and part-time positions at Detroit and Downriver area corporate fitness centers. Either the BS or BA degree is required. Current CPR Certification is also required.

   Salary: $23,825 per year plus paid overtime. There is an excellent benefits package.

Exercisejobs.com

By comparison, the following jobs were posted on the *exercisejobs.com* [http://www.exercisejobs.com/]; an online career center for fitness and exercise professionals [3]:

1. *Job Title:* **Corporate Fitness Manager**

   Company: Cardio-Kinetics, Inc.

   Location: Philadelphia/Delaware, Delaware

   Job Description: Cardio-Kinetics, Inc. is located in Newark, Delaware. We are seeking a full-time applicant to work in our corporate fitness centers in the Philadelphia, PA area. Primary responsibilities include:

   - Working with clients from 18 to 90 years of age, teaching and leading them in ways to prevent heart disease;
   - Training new staff regarding exercise ECG, flexibility, body composition, and strength testing; and
   - Leading clients with a personally-designed program based on clinical test results.

   Salary: Not indicated.

2. *Job Title:* **Exercise Physiologist**

   Company: Rippe Lifestyle Institute

   Location: Celebration, Florida

Job Description: Rippe Lifestyle Institute at Florida Hospital Celebration Health has an immediate opening for a clinical exercise physiologist. United States residency or citizenship is required. Applicants must have received the master's degree in exercise physiology or related field, and have experience in clinical exercise testing and prescription.

Salary: Not indicated.

3. *Job Title:* **Fitness and Health Promotion Manager**

   Company: Whole Health Management

   Location: Marysville, Ohio

   Job Description: Whole Health Management is an innovative organization that provides ways for the American workforce to benefit from improved wellness. We operate on-site employee healthcare programs and clinics. Presently, we seek a fitness professional for our new Scotts health center in Marysville Ohio. This person will manage, supervise, and coordinate the following duties:

   - Act as the main liaison between the fitness center and the medical services;
   - Act as main liaison between the fitness center and the client;
   - Supervise general fitness assessments, consultation, and exercise prescriptions;
   - Supervise coordinator of health promotion and special events, strength and conditioning, facility maintenance, activity classes, and sports related injuries;
   - Supervise daily operations of the fitness center;
   - Develop and maintain an effective fitness center staff, manage weekly schedules, and meetings; and
   - Coordinate the fitness center communications and bulletin boards.

The additional supervisory responsibilities include: (a) supervising 1 to 3 employees in the site, including interviewing, hiring, and training employees; (b) planning, assigning, and directing work; (c) appraising performance; rewarding and disciplining employees; and (d) addressing complaints and resolving problems. Education and experience should include a master's degree in Exercise Science, Exercise Physiology, Health Promotion, Corporate Wellness or Physical Education. Two years of fitness management experience as a Fitness Director in a corporate and wellness setting is preferred.

Salary: Not indicated.

4. *Job Title:* **Exercise Physiologist**

   Company: Cardiac Care Exercise Institute

   Location: Brooklyn, New York

   Job Description: Full-time position in Phase II cardiac rehabilitation program housed in a private medical practice. The master's degree is preferred with internship experience or with work experience in phase II cardiac rehab.

   Salary: Not mentioned.

5. *Job Title:* **Wellness Director**

   Company: YMCA of Central Maryland

   Location: Baltimore, Maryland

   Job Description: Provide direction and guidance for new YMCA facility on site of old Memorial Stadium in Baltimore, MD. The Wellness Director will oversee all the participants' health and wellness programs. Partnership with Union Memorial Hospital has on-site Sports Medicine office and a Cardio Rehabilitation and Medical Fitness Center that also requires coordination and cooperation between two organizations. Other responsibilities include:

- Hiring and supervising of fitness attendants to administer orientations;
- Assisting with training sessions of all YMCA members;
- Planning, scheduling and implementing members' involvement in aerobics programs; and
- Joining leadership team to help realize goal of YMCA to build strong kids, strong families, and strong communities.

Salary: Not mentioned.

Other jobs posted by *exercisejobs.com/* included:

1. Personal Trainer
2. Fitness Specialist/Assistant Manager
3. Fitness Sales
4. Senior Exercise Specialist
5. Exercise Physiologist
6. Outpatient Exercise Physiologist
7. Cardiac Rehab Exercise Physiologist

HealthandWellnessJobs.com

Jobs listed on the *HealthandWellnessJobs.com* Internet website [4] include the following [http://www.healthandwellnessjobs.com/]:

1. *Job Title:* **Staff Associate/Director**

   Company: University at Buffalo

   Location: Buffalo, NY

   Job Description: University at Buffalo Wellness Education Services is recruiting a Staff Associate (full-time) to fill the position of Director. This position is open to individuals who meet the following qualifications: Master's degree in the field of health education required. Doctorate in the field of health education preferred with at least 3 to 5 years of experience working in a health education setting with college students and young adults. Demonstrated experience working in an interdisciplinary team is preferred.

Salary: The salary range is $55,000 to $75,000 per year.

2. *Job Title:* **Fitness Director**

   Company: Randy Risher Fitness, Inc.

   Location: Houston, TX

   Job Description: Position is located at a 5200 acre Texas Hill Country fitness ranch/spa. The primary responsibility of the fitness director will be to design a unique fitness program at a high-end fitness ranch/spa.

   Salary: The salary is $35,000 per year with health insurance benefits, retirement plan benefits, living quarters, and meals.

AACPVR

http://www.aacvpr.org/about/affiliate_societies.cfm

The *American Association of Cardiovascular and Pulmonary Rehabilitation (AACVPR)* posts job information, too.

1. *Job Title:* **Exercise Physiologist**

   Company: Green Bay HeartCare

   Location: Green Bay, WI

   Job Description: Full-time position for an exercise physiologist available at the Cardiovascular Wellness Center. Responsibilities include all aspects of Phase III, IV, CHF and personal training fitness programs. Candidate must be able to:

   - Perform routine stress testing;
   - Recognize ECG rhythms and contraindications to exercise; and
   - Acknowledge abnormal and normal physiological responses to exercise.

Opportunities exist for various health fairs, screening events and outreach programs. The candidate must have the ability to work with all types of patients and clinic departments. The undergraduate degree in exercise physiology or related field is required. The MS/MA is preferred, however.
Salary: Note mentioned.

2. *Job Title:* **Clinical Exercise Physiologist**
   Company: Memorial Healthcare, Viroqua
   Location: Viroqua, WI
   Job Description: Full-time position in our Cardiopulmonary Diagnostics and Rehabilitation department. Candidates must have an undergraduate degree in clinical exercise physiology with an emphasis on cardiac rehabilitation. Opportunity exists to work with diverse patient population performing Phase I and II cardiac rehabilitation, GXTs and other cardiac and pulmonary evaluations and rehabilitation.
   Salary: Not mentioned.

3. *Job Title:* **Cardiology Technician**
   Company: Amery Regional Medical Center
   Location: Amery, WI
   Job Description: Part-time exercise physiologist position available, working approximately 24 hours per week. Specific requirements include:
   - Ability to work independently with little supervision;
   - Keep abreast of trends and changes in areas of responsibilities;
   - Available to work flexible schedules according to medical center needs;
   - Ability to maintain confidentiality;
   - Computer skills;
   - Excellent oral and written communication skills;

- Willingness to learn and adapt to changing environment; and
- Be a team player.

Salary: Not mentioned. Benefits package includes paid time off, health, dental, and life insurance, short and long term disability insurance, retirement plan, and competitive wages.

4. *Job Title:* **Exercise Physiologist**

   Company: University of Wisconsin Medical Foundation

   Location: Madison, WI

   Job Description: Full-time exercise physiologist position available in our Cardiology Clinic. The person hired will be responsible for:

   - Performing exercise tolerance tests under medical supervision;
   - Providing technical support for ECG department; and
   - Providing medical assessment and evaluation in the outpatient cardiology clinic.

   Candidate must have a master's degree in exercise physiology.

   Salary: Not mentioned.

ASEP Listing of Jobs

The *American Society of Exercise Physiologists* advertises jobs. The following is an example of the jobs posted on the *ASEPNewsletter* and other ASEP websites (such as the JEPonline and PEPonline):

http://www.asep.org
http://www.exercisephysiologists.com/ASEPNewsletter/index.html
http://www.asep.org/jeponline/JEPhome.php
http://faculty.css.edu/tboone2/asep/Professionalization.html

1. *Job Title:* **Wellness Program Specialist**

   Company: Westfield Group

   Location: Westfield Center, OH

   Job Description: Responsible for a variety of health and fitness activities including:

   - Assisting in the day-to-day education and exercise prescription of the Inn Club members;
   - Providing daily health and fitness screening;
   - Instructing aerobic, stretch and tone classes;
   - Providing nutritional information;
   - Helping prepare health topics for communication pieces;
   - Maintaining exercise equipment;
   - Providing health education presentations; and
   - Organizing Recreational Programming/Leagues.

   The applicant will have a bachelor's degree in exercise physiology, health promotion, athletic training, physical or health education (or related field), or comparable work experience in health, exercise and/or physiology. The applicant will have a demonstrated ability to teach exercise classes and use exercise equipment. A valid driver's license with safe driving record will be necessary as the position involves some travel. Good computer skills are also essential.

   Salary: Not mentioned.

2. *Job Title:* **Exercise Physiologist**

   Company: Washington State University Program in Health Sciences

   Job Description: Invites applications for a full-time (100%), 9-month, tenure track position at the Assistant Professor or Associate Professor level. Responsibilities include:

- Teaching graduate and undergraduate clinical exercise physiology or other related courses;
- Advising and directing graduate and undergraduate students;
- Serving as a member of the faculty team in the Clinical and Experimental Exercise Science graduate degree and the Exercise Physiology and Metabolism undergraduate degree; and
- Sustaining a clinical or basic science research program.

3. *Job Title:* **Professional Trainer Position**

   Company: LifeStyle Management

   Location: Minneapolis, MN

   Job Description: A full-time position available for an experienced and degreed professional in exercise physiology and/or athletic training. This position would require travel to alternate LifeStyle managed sites. LifeStyle Management is a progressive medically based company with multiple private/corporate sites. Excellent technical, customer service, organizational, and computer skills are a must. Applicants must have a minimum of two years experience in personal training and a certification by ASEP, ACSM, NSCA, NATA, or NASM. This position offers potential for advancement based upon performance.

4. *Job Title:* **Exercise Physiologist**

   Company: Kosciusko Community Hospital

   Job Description: Our goal is to provide customer service that exceeds the expectations of patients, physicians and the community. If you are committed to the same expectations, then we are currently seeking you as a new team member. Kosciusko has an opening in the Wellness Center for an experienced exercise physiologist. The successful candidates will posses a bachelor's degree in exercise physiology and 3 to 6 months experience in a Hospital Cardiac Rehabilitation program. The EPC board certification is preferred. KCH offers a competitive salary and benefits package.

5. *Job Title:* **Director of Exercise Physiology**

   Company: Coler-Goldwater Specialty Hospital

   Job Description: Coler-Goldwater Speciality Hospital and Nursing facility seeks a Director of Exercise Physiology interested in working in a leading rehabilitation center to play a vital role in the successful rehabilitation of our cardiac and general rehabilitation patients. The candidate's hands-on responsibilities include:

   - Patient evaluations, exercise stress testing, risk factor management, and exercise training;
   - Working with our Cardiology, Immunology and Neurology Departments to perform complex cardiopulmonary stress testing, pulmonary stress testing, spirometry and bronchospasm evaluations; and
   - Willing to open the door to research and education endeavors, which our institution finds important to remain in the forefront of rehabilitation services.

   The successful candidate must have a master's degree in exercise physiology or closely related field, strong analytical skills and a minimum of one year of clinical experience in a hospital or cardiac rehabilitation setting. BLS or ACLS certification is preferred. We offer competitive salaries and an excellent benefits package including an on-site health club.

HPCareer.net

Founded in 1999, *HPCareer.net, Inc.,* [5] has become the leader in delivering online career resources in health promotion. The advertisements help

http://www.hpcareer.net/about_p.cfm

students and college graduates in their quest for their first job or for those who seek career advancement.

HPCareer.net provides a custom advertising system, combining e-mail and the web, delivering career opportunities direct to thousands of pre-qualified candidates who meet minimum qualifications. Employers begin receiving responses to their ads by e-mail or fax in 24 hours or less. Several of the listings [http://www.hpcareer.net/jobspage.cfm] include:

- Wellness Coordinator
- Fitness Program
- Event Coordinator
- Health and Group Fitness Specialist
- Fitness Center Manager
- Fitness Specialist
- Health Fitness Specialist
- Program Manager
- Senior Health Promotion Specialist
- Health and Productivity Consultant
- Fitness Director

From the ASEP perspective, the academic major in exercise physiology is defined around "four" important healthcare components:

- health promotion
- fitness development
- cardiopulmonary rehabilitation
- athletic performance

These areas illustrate the niche job market opportunities for all Board Certified Exercise Physiologists (EPCs). However, neither the academic departments and their respective faculty nor the potential employers in each of the above

86

mentioned areas is fully aware of the academic preparation and professional development of graduates in exercise physiology. It is just a matter of time that the exercise physiology niche will be recognized throughout the public sector. This information is important and should be shared with anyone interested in exercise physiology. Concerns about the rising costs of healthcare will drive the need for alternative approaches to gain control on costs. Exercise physiologists will help relieve the rising overall costs and healthcare concerns through the implementation of safe and regular exercise programs.

Networking is Critical

Many jobs are not advertised. That is why networking is vital to locating jobs. Hence, before graduation, start the job search by talking with everyone possible about all kinds of jobs. Talk to faculty members about their contacts in specific areas of employment. It may be adult health promotion or cardiac rehabilitation or working with athletes or young children. Concentrate on speaking with friends, students, and graduates of the program. Consult with the faculty members or the department chair about alumni who may have contacts with potential employers.

Find out which internship programs are the best. Some offer a comprehensive hands-on experience. Others are more focused with specifically described job duties. Ask the department clinical coordinator and/or the preceptor in advance about mentoring. Find out if the preceptor has a history of hiring interns. Ask if the preceptor has access to other employers who hire exercise physiologists.

Advertisements

Career opportunities are advertised in newspapers, at professional meetings, in journals, in university career offices, in academic departments, and on professional web sites. In other words, there are a plethora of choices to help find the right job. Learn from your parents, co-workers, preceptors, teachers, counselors and, of course, the Internet. All this and more will be self-evident as you near completion of your academic degree. Just listen to possibilities, and be active in your search. Exercise physiology can only get hotter! In fact, by 2012, healthcare providing industries will grow very fast and employ more people than ever before.

Applying for a Job

Send the resume and cover letter directly to the person responsible for obtaining information and/or hiring the right candidate. The purpose of the resume is to get an interview. The purpose of the cover letter is to introduce the resume. Both documents must meet specific standards when applying for a job.

The **resume** summarizes personal and professional experiences such as education, hands-on laboratory skills, internship experiences, computer and software knowledge, and interests relevant to the employer. It should be no more than two pages. Place at the top of the first page your full name with academic initials (such as BA or MS), professional certifications (EPC), complete address (current and/or permanent), email address, and phone numbers (with ZIP code) where you can be reached. Add sections that highlight qualifications, academic degrees with dates, honors, awards, internship placements and a listing of professional experiences and memberships, and any other information (like community service, presentations, and publications) that is helpful for the employer to reach you or determine your qualifications for the job you are seeking.

Of course there is the layout or style and the overall appearance of the resume to consider. Make sure there are no

> **References do not need to be listed in the resume.**

typos. It should be easy to read with consistent headings with boldface, capitalization, and indentation. Both the resume and the cover letter should be printed on white or off-white quality bond paper. When the potential employer

88

requests the resume by an email attachment, be sure to attach both your cover letter and resume.

The one-page personalized **cover letter** accomplishes two purposes. First, it is written to a specific person to get his or her attention. Make sure the letter is correctly typed on high-quality paper. Learn everything you can about the employer and the organization. Second, the content of the letter explains why you are interested in the position and the institution. You might write something like:

> I was interested to read in the Duluth News that St. Luke's Hospital is looking for an exercise physiologist with experience in cardiac rehabilitation. I will receive my academic degree in exercise physiology from The College of St. Scholastica in May, and I am eager to be considered for the position.

or

> Dr. Larry Dargan told me that the Guidant Corporation will be hiring an exercise physiologist with research experience. I am writing to express my interest in the position. I will graduate in July from The College of St. Scholastica Department of Exercise Physiology in July with a master's degree in exercise physiology.

You may also want to emphasize parts of your academic and hands-on experiences. For example, you might write:

> As my enclosed resume indicates, I have had significant research experience using the Medical Graphics CardiO2 metabolic analyzer as an intern exercise physiologist at Cardiovascular Consultants. In addition, during the four months I was at CC, I was responsible for the statistical analysis of the cardiovascular data. My academic work at St. Scholastica and the internship research opportunities have impressed upon me the value of practicing exercise physiology in a research based cardiac rehabilitation hospital. I am impressed with the research presented at the *American Society of Exercise Physiologists* this past April, and I feel that your institution provides the best professional opportunities for ongoing work."

Finish the letter by indicating an interest in an interview, and that you will follow up with a phone call.

Interview Techniques

The interview is vital to getting a job. The following points should be thoroughly considered before the interview. *First,* preparation is absolutely required. Find out everything possible from every source conceivable about the employer (e.g., friends, libraries, colleagues, brochures, contacts, and websites). *Second,* have a good sense of why you want the job. Have answers to the following questions:

1. Tell me a little about yourself, recent jobs, and how you plan to contribute to the profession.
2. Why did you to become an exercise physiologist?
3. Why are you specializing in cardiac rehabilitation?
4. How would you describe your education from St. Scholastica?
5. Do you believe research is important?
6. What professional organizations do you belong to?
7. What are your professional strengths and weaknesses?
8. How would your strengths help us?
9. Do you see yourself continuing in exercise physiology?
10. What are your leadership skills?
11. What are your salary requirements?
12. Why should St. Luke's hire you?

Third, arrive at least 10 minutes early to the interview. *Fourth,* dress appropriately and be professional (e.g., wear a suit, tie, sports coat, slacks, and polished footwear). *Fifth,* be enthusiastic and positive about past experiences. *Sixth,* practice and practice answering the questions. Use a friend or a mentor.

In addition to the information in this chapter, you will want to consult other sources. Consider reading the Student Affairs Career Services Online articles that address many of the points in this chapter. Use the following URL:

http://www.ub-careers.buffalo.edu/career/oco/cpp/student/jobsrch.shtml

Similarly, you will want to check the ASEP job search information posted on the following URL:

| **http://www.asep.org/Advertisement.php** |

Aging of the Population

With the aging of the population, nursing care facilities, in particular, are expected to grow tremendously. Exercise physiologists will increasingly become part of the front line staff responsible for directing and managing the care for aging or disabled residents of care facilities. Patients in these facilities need an exercise physiologist who is familiar with exercise programs, prescriptions, and benefits of participation. Exercise physiologists will assess health and fitness of the residents, develop exercise programs, supervise other staff not qualified to prescribe exercise to rehabilitate clients of different physical conditions. Exercise physiologists in these settings will need to have good judgment, must be able to work independently, and are good candidates for management and leadership positions. Those with several years of experience can either be promoted within their work or they can enter a related field.

Just decades ago, exercise physiologists could not imagine that "exercise as medicine" would be as popular as it is today. Board certified exercise physiologists will have their foot in the door to getting a specialty certification that will also enhance career opportunities. For example, an "aging certification" or an "obesity certification" and, of course, others allow for increase career opportunities in many different roles and settings in the healthcare field.

The rapid changes in healthcare environments will lead to "new thinking" and "new employment opportunities" driven by the healthcare needs of the public sector. Exercise physiologists with a scientific background in the physiology of aging will be highly valued as leaders in the field.

Part Three

Professionalism

If there is no struggle, there is no progress – Frederick Douglass

Do not lose courage in considering your own imperfections, but instantly set about remedying them. – St. Francis de Sales

Chapter Nine

Fundamentals of Professionalism

Exercise physiologists can no longer ignore the moral impact of their lack of leadership in professionalism, ethics, and accreditation responsibilities that guide other healthcare professions.

While cultivating the values of professionalism is not a new concept in healthcare professions that are well established, it is a new area of discussion and analysis among exercise physiologists [1-2]. Much of this discussion is led by the ASEP leaders. They are concerned about the professional development of exercise physiology. This is why they built the ASEP professional infrastructure. Now, it is just a matter of time, commitment, and courage to ensure the credibility of exercise physiologists as healthcare professionals.

In general, a "profession" is defined as having a specific knowledge area with associated abilities that are applied to the welfare of the public. Exercise physiology is a profession because exercise physiologists have a scientific body of knowledge that has been systematically research and applied to healthcare activities that are passed on to students, athletes, and clients in the public sector. This definition is also consistent with the following criteria for a profession [3-4]:

1. A body of knowledge on which skills and services are based;
2. An ability to deliver a unique service to the public sector;
3. Standardized college education;
4. Control of standards of practice;
5. Member responsibility and accountability for their actions;
6. Career commitment by members; and
7. Independent function.

Because "exercise" is central to health and wellness, exercise physiology has important healthcare qualities. This is recognized because the definition of "a healthcare profession" is the prevention, treatment, and management of illness. Exercise physiology is therefore a healthcare profession since "exercise" helps to prevent, treat, and manage illness [5-6].

In other words, by comparison, personal training cannot be identified as a profession since it neither belongs to nor practices as a profession. The desire of exercise physiologists during the early 21st century to control their body of knowledge and its application to society's needs is probably much like the work of nursing or physical therapy decades ago. It is not surprising that this is a huge step in the direction of professionalism. Other steps include the intellectual responsibility of learning and conveying the unique health and fitness insights, rehabilitation concepts, and sports training ideas of exercise physiology to the public sector.

Exercise Physiologists are Professionals

Exercise physiologists behave as professionals. Three important criteria support this point. First, they know the best fitness program for their clients. Their work is based on scientific information regarding healthcare, fitness, rehabilitation, and sports training issues. Second, they have their own professional organization to protect the autonomy of its members through accreditation, board certification, and (eventually) licensure. Third, board certified exercise physiologists are competent in applying their shared knowledge to benefit society.

Professionalism

Professionalism is defined as the commitment to one's work and the orientation towards service rather than personal profit. Professionalization is the degree to which the characteristics of the ideal profession are demonstrated in the everyday functions of its members. It is a process that is ongoing.

As members of an occupation commit to being a profession, the level of professionalism rises. The professionalization of the occupation moves closer to the professional status that defines the members of the profession. Professionalism that is at the heart of the

> The idea of being committed to one's work is similar to a sense of calling.

emerging profession. Members must come to understand what it means to them. Given the belief that exercise physiology is evolving as a profession, and given that professions require their members to demonstrate professionalism, it is necessary that exercise physiologists understand clearly what exercise physiology professionalism entails. If they look the other way, the professionalization of exercise physiology will be prolonged unnecessarily.

If professionalism is considered as important as research, then exercise physiologists will develop controls over their professional development. Unfortunately, this point is exactly what has been missing for decades. No one emphasized the importance of exercise physiology as a "calling" in its application to the public sector. It was and continues to be an occupation to many exercise physiologists, particularly those with the doctorate degree. That is, the academic exercise physiologist, at least those privileged with both position and reasonably good to excellent financial incentives, often conform to teaching their courses as they were taught. Many do not appear interested in professional development, especially if it takes them from their research efforts and goals.

While exercise physiologists stand at the forefront of important integration into healthcare, they need a better understanding of their responsibilities regarding professional development. The effect of this situation is to encourage exercise physiologists to stop "burying their heads in the sand." The window of opportunity is open with significant improvement in professional status and financial reward. One needs only to search the Internet which readily yields hundreds of articles and books that speak to the importance of "exercise as medicine." Furthermore, the exercise physiologist is the only healthcare profession with the word "exercise" in its title.

Chapter Ten

Exercise Physiology Body of Knowledge

The interconnectedness of all information engages most exercise physiologists beyond their wildest expectations.

The primary reason for studying exercise physiology has always been to better understand human performance and athletics. However, given the value of exercise in promoting health, it was not long before exercise physiologists were researching the benefits of exercise in helping to modify risk factors for obesity and coronary artery disease.

Although physical activity and exercise training are still at the center of the

> **The body of knowledge unique to exercise physiology is the result of decades of research.**

development of exercise physiology, the study of acute and chronic adaptations of exercise training is no longer *the* definition of exercise physiology.

Today, exercise physiology is considered a healthcare profession. Not surprisingly, this thinking resulted from the careful analysis of the positive effects of regular exercise on numerous healthcare issues and concerns. Hence, while many graduates still locate jobs in athletics, corporate fitness, recreational and fitness programs, and cardiac rehabilitation programs, the academic course work and hands-on experiences encourage a much broader definition of exercise physiology.

"Exercise as therapy" is obvious throughout the scientific literature [1]. The question is this: "Who is best educated to deliver the preventive strategies that focus on exercise to benefit the public?" From the exercise physiologist's point of view, the answer is of course the "Exercise Physiologists." They have the understanding of anatomy, physiology, and the metabolic responses to exercise and training along with changes in body composition and lifestyle modifications necessary to prevent and/or postpone cardiovascular diseases and dysfunctions. They also understand the effects of exercise on bone remodeling, the management strategies for handling stress at work and in life, and the use of exercise in rehabilitation from different diseases and dysfunctions. Much of this information is taught in undergraduate courses such as:

- Nutrition and Exercise
- Kinesiology (Anatomy)
- Fitness Assessment
- Exercise Prescription
- Statistics
- Scientific Writing
- Exercise and Aging
- Exercise Biochemistry
- Cardiovascular Physiology
- Psychophysiology
- Cardiac Rehabilitation
- Applied Physiology
- Advanced Exercise Physiology
- Exercise Stress Testing
- Exercise ECG
- Exercise Immunology
- Exercise in Health and Disease

Most exercise physiologists understand and value the interconnectedness of different academic courses and, therefore, are constantly in promotion of the exercise physiology as a healthcare profession. This is based on their assumption that the body's "interconnectedness" is greater than its sum of parts. As a result of this thinking, exercise physiologists know that competence in just exercise training will not serve the client well when the management of lifestyle issues and concerns should also embrace the totality of the mind-body factors (such as the negative effects of stress on the body). It is the integrated application of the body of knowledge that defines the exercise physiology professional.

Exercise Physiology
Bioenergetics
The conversion of carbohydrates, fats, and proteins into a biologically usable form of energy is termed bioenergetics. Extracting energy from foodstuffs is necessary to maintain cellular activities at rest and during exercise. Muscle cells can produce "energy" by a combination of three metabolic pathways [2]:

1. Making adenosine triphosphate (ATP) by phosphocreatine (PC) breakdown (e.g., PC = P + C where P is donated to ADP to form ATP);
2. Making ATP by the degradation of glucose or glycogen to pyruvic acid (called glycolysis); and
3. Making ATP within the mitochondria (i.e., more specifically, the electron transport system that is located within the mitochondria).

The making of ATP by the PC pathway and glycolysis does not require oxygen and, thus is termed anaerobic. The making of ATP in the mitochondria requires the use of oxygen, which is called aerobic. To understand anaerobic and aerobic metabolism, students are first taught the steps of glycolysis. They realize that if oxygen is available at the mitochondria, then the products of glycolysis results in the making ATP. This view of glycolysis can be considered "aerobic glycolysis" even though glycolysis *per se* does not use oxygen. Conversely, if there is not adequate oxygen at the cell level, then the products of glycolysis results in the formation of lactic acid. When this happens, the steps from glucose to pyruvic acid, which gets converted to lactic acid can be referred to as anaerobic glycolysis.

Exercise Metabolism

Exercise challenges the bioenergetic pathways to increase oxygen consumption some 20 times above the expenditure at rest. The purpose of the increase in oxygen is to increase ATP production within the muscles to meet the metabolic demand of increased muscle contraction during exercise. Trained athletes are able to meet the cellular oxygen needs immediately during the first few minutes of exercise. As a result, they accumulate a smaller oxygen deficit when compared to untrained athletes. Following exercise, oxygen consumption remains elevated for several minutes depending upon the intensity of the exercise. The excess oxygen consumption above resting is frequently termed oxygen debt.

High-intensity exercise that lasts less than 10 seconds uses primarily anaerobic metabolic pathways to produce ATP. Intense exercise lasting more than 20 seconds relies more on anaerobic glycolysis to produce ATP. High-intensity exercise longer than 45 seconds requires the use of the ATP-PC system, glycolysis, and the aerobic system (i.e., Krebs cycle and the electron transport system). However, if exercise is greater than 10 minutes at a relative moderate heart rate intensity (60% of maximum), the energy source comes primarily from aerobic metabolism.

The measurement of aerobic metabolism or aerobic power either during submaximal or maximal workloads, is termed oxygen consumption (VO_2) or maximum oxygen consumption (VO_2 max), respectively. The latter measurement is a valid analysis of cardiovascular fitness. Exercise physiologists use it in conjunction with a treadmill or a cycle ergometer to measure the ability of the oxygen transport system to deliver oxygen to the contracting muscles. The test also represents the ability of the muscles to use oxygen and to produce ATP aerobically.

With a metabolic cart, exercise physiologists can estimate the percent contribution of carbohydrate or fat in the making of energy for muscle contraction. Knowing the interaction and selection of fuel during exercise at different heart rates and duration of exercise allows for a better understanding of how to train athletes in different sports. The information also identifies the intensity of effort that is best fueled by fat metabolism to decrease body fat. Also, the use of the metabolic cart and a standard laboratory bike or treadmill allows for the measurement of energy expenditure during exercise allows for the calculation of exercise efficiency (or economy) and factors that affect it.

Cardiovascular Responses to Exercise

To understand oxygen consumption, exercise physiologists determine cardiac output (Q), which is the product of heart rate (HR) and stroke volume (SV). Exercise causes HR and SV to increase and, therefore, Q is increased. As a result, there is an increase in oxygen transported to the muscles. The increased oxygen is used to make more ATP for increased muscle contraction [2].

When the volume of blood pumped by the heart per minute (cardiac output, Q) is large, it can be useful in identifying the trained subject from the untrained. This is true because heart rate is essentially the same for the trained and untrained subjects during maximum exercise. This leaves the SV response as the responsible variable for ensuring that a larger quantity of blood (Q) is delivered to the muscles with an elevated oxygen demand. There are other variables that influence SV (such as preload, end-diastolic volume, and ventricular contractility), but you will study them much later in exercise physiology.

Other important responses and adaptations to exercise include changes in arteriovenous oxygen content (a-vO_2 diff). Using the Fick equation, (VO_2 = Q x a-vO_2 diff), exercise physiologists can calculate the amount of oxygen that is used by the muscles for contraction. The increase in VO_2 that is directly related to the increase in oxidative production of ATP by skeletal muscle is a result of several factors including, but not limited to: (1) structural and chemical changes in the skeletal muscle; and (2) a redistribution of an increase in blood flow to skeletal muscle during exercise.

103

Respiratory Responses to Exercise

In addition to understanding the mechanics of breathing, diffusion of gases, and ventilation-perfusion relationships, exercise physiologists must also understand the regulation of pulmonary gas exchange during rest and exercise. The transport of oxygen and carbon dioxide in the blood, the oxyhemoglobin dissociation curve, and oxygen transport in skeletal muscle fibers are vital topics in understanding the cardiorespiratory response during exercise.

Ventilatory control during submaximal and heavy exercise is an area of intense research. Exercise physiologists recognize that the increase in ventilation during submaximal exercise is due to the interaction of neural and humoral input to the respiratory control center. During heavy exercise, there is a strong relationship between the rise in blood lactate and the nonlinear rise in ventilation. Exercise physiologists are also active in researching the controversy over whether the lungs limit maximal exercise performance.

Temperature Regulation

The regulation of core temperature is critical to normal cellular structure and metabolic pathways during exercise. Exercise physiologists must understand temperature regulation during exercise to prevent overheating or overcooling. Measurement of deep-body temperature is accomplished by placing thermistors on the skin at different locations. Heat loss from the body occurs by radiation, conduction, convection, and/or evaporation. Each method is important, especially heat loss by evaporation during exercise in a hot environment. The rate of evaporation is dependent upon temperature and relative humidity, convective currents around the body, and the amount of skin exposed to the environment.

Exercise physiologists are interested in gender and age differences in thermoregulation during exercise. They want to know if aging impairs ability to thermoregulate and exercise in a hot environment. And, similarly, does the lack of heat acclimatization in older subjects decrease thermoregulation with age? What is heat acclimatization? What does it have to do with an increased plasma volume, earlier onset of sweating, higher sweat rate, decreased salt loss in sweat, and a reduced skin blood flow? Similarly, exercise physiologists are interested in the physiological changes that occur during exercise in a cold environment.

Principles of Training

The three principles of cardiorespiratory training are: (a) overload, (b) specificity, and (c) reversibility [3]. Overload refers to the training effect occurs when tissue is challenged with intensity, frequency, and duration of exercise to which it is unaccustomed. The principle of specificity indicates that the training effect is limited to the muscles, issues, and systems involved in the activity. Aerobic training results in an increase in mitochondria and capillaries within the muscle fibers. Weight training, on the other hand, increases the size and strength of the muscles.

Exercises that require large muscle mass (such as cycling, cross-country skiing, jogging, running, and swimming) for 30 to 60 minutes three times a week result in an increase in VO_2 max. When the intensity of aerobic training is between 50% and 75% of VO_2 max, there is an increase on average of 15%. About 50% of the increase in VO_2 max is directly related to the increase in SV, while a-vO_2 diff is responsible for the other 50%. The increase in SV is the result of the increase in end-diastolic volume (i.e., the volume of blood in the ventricles before contraction), the increase in the strength of ventricular contraction, and the decrease in total peripheral resistance (SVR).

The increased capacity of the muscles to extract more oxygen is a function of an increase in capillary density that accommodates the increase in muscle blood flow while also slowing the red blood cell transit time through the muscle tissue. The latter adaptation increases the diffusion time for oxygen from hemoglobin to the mitochondria in the muscles. The increase in the number of mitochondria allows for an increase in the development of ATP (energy) for muscle contraction. This adaptation is also related to the increases in the mitochondria enzymes involved in oxidative metabolism.

105

Exercise physiologists are also interested in the physiology of increased strength. Neuromuscular adaptations are particularly important to the increase in strength and muscle endurance. This is one of the benefits of weight training, which enhances specific neural adaptations that increased the activation of motor units. Strength training also increases the size of the muscle fibers, which is correlated with the increase in strength. The increase in cross-sectional area (hypertrophy) of existing fibers is due to the enlargement of the existing muscle fibers (hypertrophy), not to an increase in the number of fibers (hyperplasia).

Anatomy

The study of the structure of the human body and the relationships of the anatomical parts to each other is defined as anatomy [4]. Knowledge of the bony and muscular structures of the body is imperative for all exercise physiologists. It is necessary in order to understand the control or movement of the body at rest or during sports. Also, knowledge of anatomy is important for proper rehabilitation after disease or dysfunction. How else would a person know which muscles to develop and which exercises are the best to perform? Likewise, if an exercise physiologist is interested in developing a greater range of motion across selected joints, which exercises should be used and why? Which exercises would be useful, wasteful, or even dangerous?

Muscle tissue is composed of specialized cells called fibers that function by contraction to product motion across a joint. The fibers are grouped in bundles known as fasciculi that are bound together by fascia to form muscles. When nerve cells transmit impulses to the muscles, they produce movement of the body parts. For example, when a person decides to flex the left elbow (i.e., bring the hand towards the face), electrical impulses are sent from the right side of the brain down the spinal cord to a peripheral nerves that signal the elbow flexors to contract (shorten).

The vocabulary of anatomy is not all that difficult, but it is extensive. In nearly all instances, the study of anatomy takes time for a thorough analysis and

106

application. For example, regarding the biceps brachii, a two-headed muscle in the arm, it is important to know the origin, insertion, and functions. This requires memorization reinforced by insight and understanding. Aside from learning directional terms, like anterior, posterior, lateral, medial, superior, and inferior, it is the responsibility of the exercise physiologist to know the major skeletal muscles (also known as voluntary muscles) by name and function.

If you are interested in helping others to keep their muscles strong, analyzing human movement patterns, or developing strength and flexibility programs for athletes and others, then exercise physiology is the right career for you. There is one important consideration, however. Not all academic programs, especially the non-exercise physiology programs like kinesiology, non-accredited exercise science, and human performance, teach comprehensive functional anatomy. This is not the case with the ASEP accredited exercise physiology programs. They understand the importance of teaching applied anatomy (structure) and integrating it with exercise physiology (function).

In the near future, there will be an even greater emphasis placed on anatomy and its application by exercise physiologists. As mentioned, members of the ASEP Board of Accreditation believe that anatomy of the human body is an essential course of study. As a result, the ASEP Board of Certification has incorporated a significant number of anatomy questions into the "Exercise Physiologist Certified" (EPC) exam. The ASEP leadership understands that being flexible means having the ability to use the muscles through a range of performance.

Athletes have many questions about the benefits of stretching. Exercise physiologists ask the same questions. For example, why is staying flexible important? How can you increase flexibility? How does a greater range of motion decrease injuries? How often should you stretch? Are there certain flexibility exercises better than others? Are there dangerous and even useless flexibility exercises?

Biomechanics

The mechanical principles of human movement helps exercise physiologists understand the physics of forces and effects. Many of the problems in the public sector are self-induced, given the lack of knowledge regarding how to move the body safely and correctly. Other problems deal more directly with recreational participants and/or athletes who exercise too hard. The study of biomechanics helps students of exercise physiology apply biomechanical principles to specific problems that deal primarily with teaching and developing athletic skills [5].

The integration of anatomical concepts with biomechanical problems is useful in understanding human movement and athletic performances. Students interested in exercise physiology will learn that motion is either linear (a straight-line path) or curvilinear (a curved path). Perhaps it should be pointed out that this section is only a basic statement of the concepts of biomechanics. Since human movement is more than physiological or anatomical, students must study the enormous contribution from biomechanics.

The professional applications of biomechanics are particularly important in terms of cause-and-effect relationships. The process itself requires qualitative and quantitative analyses of human motion. The assignment of numbers and units (i.e., quantification) to specific body conditions is critical to describing linear and angular displacements. The resolution of vectors, use of cinematographic equipment, along with describing motion in terms of speed, velocity, and acceleration are all part of the work of the exercise physiologist who integrates biomechanics with a comprehensive analysis of human performance. This is also true for analysis of parabolic motion (i.e., aerial trajectories).

Biomechanical research is also useful in the analysis of sports footwear (shoes), shoe inserts, and a variety of other athletic wear and equipment that may result in an improvement in performance. The biomechanical evaluation of rehabilitation equipment is useful in determining whether prostheses and wheelchairs are designed as they should be. Many of these professional opportunities include positions in industry, government, academia, and private healthcare.

Cardiac Rehabilitation

During the 1970s, exercise physiologists were responsible for prescribing exercise to rehabilitate patients with coronary artery disease. The majority of the patients referred to programs for "cardiac rehabilitation" have had one or more myocardial infarctions (heart attacks). Exercise physiologists have worked for decades with the medical community to strengthen the cardiovascular system of cardiac patients [6].

Many of the original programs were university-based outpatient rehabilitation for heart patients. Such programs are known today as Phase III cardiac rehabilitation. Over the past 40 years of systematically testing and exercising patients with heart attacks, patients with chest pain, and heart transplant patients, most exercise physiologists understand that the rehabilitation programs result in significant changes in the muscles to extract more oxygen during exercise. The disease itself may not go away, but the patients do appear to acquire increase stamina to do more work. This is especially important because it encourages the patients to think that life can (and does) go on after a heart attack.

Exercise physiologists also test and rehabilitate a variety of patients with cardiac and pulmonary related diseases and dysfunctions. Patients are also now referred to such programs following cardiac surgery. The positive effects of exercise are accepted by a high percent of the medical and healthcare community. And, they have come to recognize the academic specialization that exercise physiologists bring to the clinical setting.

Lifestyle (risk factor) management is in itself a field of increasing opportunity, particularly for exercise physiologists who look to work with the public in the prevention and/or management of diseases resulting from lifestyle choices. The opportunity for work in cardiac and/or pulmonary rehabilitation is good to excellent in the near future. The question is whether the non-doctorate exercise physiologists are likely to continue to follow the model of being hired by hospitals or whether they will establish their own outpatient rehabilitation programs. In the latter case, the business-oriented exercise physiologist will work with the medical doctor to oversee graded exercise testing for legal reasons and be physically at the site where exercise is taking place. Most exercise physiologists believe that patients will gladly pay out of pocket for such services. And, most certainly, they will want the supervision and guidance of exercise physiology professionals who are board certified.

Exercise Testing and Prescription

The prescription for how hard (intensity), how long (duration), and how often (frequency) an individual should exercise depends entirely on the knowledge gained from a "graded exercise test." Some years ago, the *[test]* was called a "stress test" because it was viewed that the subject was being "stressed" throughout the duration of the test by increasing the grade and speed of the treadmill [7]. It is probably more common to speak of the test today as a "graded exercise test." Of course, this means exactly the same since "to grade" or "to push" a subject requires either raising the speed of the test or the percent elevation and, on occasion, both at the same moment.

By stressing the subject's cardiovascular system, meaning, primarily the subject's heart rate and blood pressure responses to increasing workloads, the exercise physiologist determines the subject's overall metabolic capacity for work (i.e., oxygen consumption, VO_2). If the subject's capacity is high for using oxygen, it is a good sign. If the value is low, the subject may expect to benefit from regular exercise.

In general, it is important that heart patients are tested for two reasons. First, they gain a sense of what is possible, physically speaking, and how much work they can do before experiencing a reduction in coronary blood flow and the onset of chest pain. Such information about the heart is important. It helps the patient to overcome feelings that life is over. Second, exercise physiologists use

110

the information to prescribe exercise that is safe and beneficial. The patient's heart rate response is used as an objective guide to safe exercise. This is why the patient's heart rate and blood pressure are measured and evaluated.

The Cardiovascular Profile

Integration of the graded exercise test data with other cardiovascular data is unique to the exercise physiologist's career opportunities. Few, if any, members of other healthcare professions engage in the same supervision and analysis. This is why the "cardiovascular profile" is so important. Results from the analysis of physiological data such as heart rate (HR), blood pressure (BP), double product (DP, a measure of the work of the heart), mean arterial pressure (MAP), systemic vascular resistance (SVR), cardiac output (Q), stroke volume (SV), tissue extraction of oxygen (arteriovenous oxygen difference, a-vO$_2$ diff), and other variables allow for numerous assessments and implications regarding aerobic and other metabolic functions at rest and during exercise [8].

The cardiovascular profile is frequently done as the subject's electrocardiographic (ECG) readings are carried out. This allows the exercise physiologist the opportunity to know when the exercise should be terminated or when certain electrical conditions of the heart require special attention by the medical doctor. Hence, exercise physiologists must know how to put electrodes on a subject correctly, operate the ECG machine without error, and know when to stop the test based on the subject's ECG response to different stages of the test.

Exercise Nutrition

Exercise physiologists synthesize scientific data from many academic sources. Sports nutrition [9] is a discipline that focuses on sound nutrition principles and concepts. In fact, contrary to the view of some sports nutritionists, it is not about sports supplements or performance-enhancing substances or, at least, it should not be. Many exercise physiologists believe that sports nutrition is important to the advancement of sports, exercise training, and competition. Exercise is not possible without energy for muscle contraction. Energy comes from the metabolism of carbohydrates, lipids, and proteins. Aside from the role of each in fueling human motion, they maintain the body's structural and functional integrity. Carbohydrates serve two very important roles in cellular metabolism:

1. They are the primary fuel source during high-intensity exercise.
2. Carbohydrate byproducts help to facilitate the metabolism of fat.

Fat (lipid) constitutes the primary cellular fuel for low-intensity, long duration exercise. Protein is used during strenuous exercise of long duration. It becomes an even more important fuel source when muscle and liver glycogen reserves are depleted. Unlike the very high contributions of carbohydrates and fats during exercise, the contribution of protein is usually around 10% to 15% of the total energy requirement.

While the role of water soluble vitamins is linked to metabolic reactions that release energy, vitamins contain no useful energy in metabolism that allows for muscle contraction. Vitamin supplementation is not recommended. It does not improve exercise or even the potential to train harder. Calcium, an important mineral, significantly influences bone remodeling. Regular exercise helps to slow the impact of various risk factors for osteoporosis, such as sedentary lifestyle, early menopause, cigarette smoking, and alcohol abuse.

What is important in exercise training is the formation of energy from anaerobic and aerobic metabolism. Exercise physiologists understand the influence of intensity of exercise on metabolism, the fuel substrate usage under different types of exercise and intensities, and the carbohydrate and fat-burning adaptations within skeletal muscle with aerobic and anaerobic training. They can determine the energy expended at rest or during exercise by measuring respiratory exchange ratio (RER). Understanding thermoregulation, environmental stress during exercise in the heat, and changes in body weight and water loss during exercise are part of the role of the exercise physiologist in avoiding training problems.

Testimonials and endorsements from sports nutritionists and various organizations tied to the sports industry argue for the need of performance-enhancing substances to perform well. The ASEP leaders do not believe in the use of sports supplements in athletics. They think it is cheating. Helping athletics understand energy balance, exercise, and weight control by testing athletes in laboratories, assessing body composition, and sport-specific nutritional observations are all important roles of the exercise physiologist.

Each of these areas of study can be measured and improved with appropriate types of exercise and advice. Now that the sports supplement boom has been underway with an increasing influence on athletes, the need for scientifically correct information is very high. Every day, there are more and more young people and athletes who believe it is necessary to consume sports supplements to win or to level the playing field. This is not likely to be good for the profession of exercise physiology or athletics.

Health and Fitness

Health is a multifaceted state of mind and body. It is generally defined as freedom from disease. That is, to be healthy, a person does not have cancer or cardiovascular disease. Using this definition, it is important not to get sick. Exercise is one way to stay healthy and physically fit. But, it is important to remember that fitness by itself is not equal to being healthy. A person can run a marathon and have cancer. And, of course, a person does not have to run a marathon to be healthy. Perhaps, it is best to conclude that it is a good objective to be a healthy person who is physically fit.

Exercise physiologists can help design sound and safe exercise programs involving running, cycling, and other aerobic forms of exercise [10]. The benefits range from increased cardiorespiratory endurance, muscular fitness, and flexibility. Each of the components of fitness can be measured and systematically developed. Exercisers can be taught to cross train (i.e., combining aerobic and anaerobic forms of exercise). Using light hand weights during aerobic work or lifting weights to build strength and lean muscle tissue are recommended. And, the exercise does not have to be exhausting or painful. Low to moderate intensity is sufficient to benefit most people.

Exercise physiologists are experts in the "how to" exercise safely, what to do before you begin, the right way to warm up, how to minimize the effects of hot and humid weather, the safe way to exercise in cold weather, the identification of flexibility exercises that are safe and why, and recommendations regarding fitness and exercise-related concerns. They recognize that the type and kind of exercise to start with can be intimidating at many levels. They understand that exercisers should be periodically evaluated to ensure that the technology is right for the consumer, that the industry is not taking advantage of the consumer, and that the medical advances in services and specialists are recognized to increase quality of services and costs.

For many people, news of medical miracles and other healthcare breakthroughs provides the quick-fix answer to their healthcare problems. For example, why would a person exercise to burn extra calories when exercise and dieting are believed to work better? Why would a person exercise when surgery can produce faster results? The last decade of surgical alternatives to dieting and exercising to correct obesity flies in the face of common sense. Americans are learning the importance of exercise in their healthcare plans. The influence of the supplement industry and the commercialization of healthcare have created volumes of misinformation about health and fitness:

1. Should I take this supplement?
2. Should I exercise?
3. If I should exercise, it is better to do it in the morning, right?
4. Which is faster? The supplement or exercise!
5. Do the sports supplements really work?
6. What is the cost-benefit ratio for the supplements vs. exercise training?

Statistics and Research Designs

All exercise physiologists are required to be knowledgeable in statistics and research designs, not to mention critical thinking skills that are important to understanding whether the authors of a research paper made the right conclusions. Statistical analysis allows for a non-biased statement of certain findings [11]. Whether it is a t-test or an analysis of variance with repeated measures, when applied correctly, exercise physiologists are clearly part of the scientific circle of advanced knowledge. They know when the research design is questionable or when the use of statistics is incorrectly applied (perhaps, to promote a product). If the findings are not correct, there must be a reason for the argument presented by the authors. If it is determined that the authors put a spin on the analysis of the data to result in certain findings, then the article can and should be dismissed as nothing more than an advertisement. If it is determined that the findings are supported by the statistical analysis and data in the study, then the views of the authors should be acknowledged as a significant contribution to the topic in question.

Psychophysiology of Health and Exercise

The effects of stress and anxiety on a client's work and personal relationships are huge [12]. Exercise physiologists teach clients to manage stress levels. They help them deal with the mind-body changes such as:

> Stress causes the excretion of steroid hormones, especially cortisol, which mobilizes glucose (an energy substrate) to produce energy for muscle contraction. In basic terms, the "stress response" is to position the body in a fight or flight opportunity to either deal with the stress or to get away from the stress. Unfortunately, the response also suppresses the immune system and its response. Epinephrine is secreted, which increases cardiac output and blood flow to the muscles to ensure that oxygen is available to metabolism the glucose for energy. Norepinephrine increases mental alertness. It also helps to ensure that the muscles get adequate blood flow by constricting vessels to tissues that do not need to be as active. In time, if stress is left unmanaged, the body begins to fail to adapt correctly. This can set the stage for pathological changes in the body.

Exercise physiologists can help their clients manage stress by introducing them to a few basic stress reduction techniques:

- Plan ahead and avoid unnecessary stressful situations.
- Develop a balance in work and recreation.
- Prioritize personal and professional responsibilities and obligations.
- Simplify life through self-help strategies and positive thinking.
- Use various relaxation procedures (such as imagery, deep breathing, and/or progressive relaxation) to fully relax the mind and body.
- Exercise regularly with the intention to improve your overall quality of life.
- Take control of your life.

Chapter Eleven

Exercise Physiology Research

In the past, exercise physiology was viewed as specialists of the exercise leader kind. Now it is commonly accepted that research designs, statistical applications, and scientific thinking are at the heart of the profession.
-- Chacie Henderson

Research is a systematic analysis of existing knowledge and the discovery of new knowledge. The goal is to validate or refine knowledge and develop new knowledge. Exercise physiologists engage in research to better understand phenomena important to the profession of exercise physiology. It is through research that they develop a strong scientific base for understanding fitness, health and wellness promotion, rehabilitation, and sports training. Because exercise physiology is a healthcare profession, it is important that the practice of exercise physiology is based on scientific knowledge, code of ethics, board certification, and a standards of practice.

Experimental Research

When exercise physiologists read that a sports massage prior to exercise will increase running efficiency, their first instinct is to design a study, collect data, analyze the data statistically and, then, write a research report that concludes objectively whether or not a sports massage lowers submaximal VO_2. It is a formal and objective process used by exercise physiologists, scientists, and other research professionals throughout the world.

Although there are different research designs published throughout the literature, exercise physiologists use predominately the experimental design that includes the manipulation of a treatment variable (such as, sports massage). This method of collecting and analyzing data is used to make decisions in everyday practice of exercise physiology.

Professors in academic settings are expected to engage in research and presentation of their findings at professional meetings. Of course, they are expected to publish the findings in scientific and professional journals. Increasingly, many non-doctorate prepared exercise physiologists are routinely reading research journal articles, carrying out quality research projects, and translating their findings into healthcare policy.

Abstract Examples of Research by Exercise Physiologists

1. *Authors:* L. Birnbaum and C. Hedlund

   Title: The Oxygen Cost of Walking With an Artifically Immobilized Knee With and Without a Shoe-Lift

   Publication: Journal of Exercise Physiologyonline (Vol 1 No 1, 1998)

   Abstract: The purpose of this study was to determine the oxygen cost (VO_2) of walking with and without a shoe-lift on the contralateral (i.e., opposite) foot of an immobilized extended knee. Cardiac output (Q) and related cardiorespiratory measurements were also analyzed to determine the effect of a shoe-lift on central (heart rate, HR; stroke volume, SV) and peripheral (arteriovenous oxygen difference, a-vO_2 diff) components of VO_2. Seven (six female, one male) subjects participated in the study. None of the subjects was on medication, and none had any known cardiopulmonary or musculoskeletal disorders. The Medical Graphics CPX/D metabolic analyzer was used to determine breath-by-breath VO_2 in ml/kg/min, which was converted to oxygen cost (ml/kg/m). The shoe-lift had no significant ($p>0.05$) effect on oxygen rate (i.e., VO_2 l/min or ml/kg/min) or oxygen cost (ml/kg/m). There were no significant differences in the volume of carbon dioxide produced (VCO_2), respiratory exchange ratio (RER), expired ventilaton (V_e), tidal volume (V_t), and frequency of breath (F_b). There were no statistically significant differences in HR, SV, Q, a-vO_2 diff, and systemic vascular resistance (SVR) between the two walking sessions with and without a shoe-lift. The results of the study indicate that a shoe-lift added to the contralateral foot of an immobilized extended knee has no effect on oxygen cost during walking and, therefore, does not improve walking economy [1].

2. *Authors:* T. Boone and J. DeWeese

Title: The Effect of Psychophysiologic Self-Regulation on Running Economy

Publication: Journal of Exercise Physiologyonline (Vol 1 No 1, 1998)

Abstract: The purpose of this study was to determine the physiological effects of eliciting the relaxation response during exercise. Nine adult females volunteered to participate in this study. The subjects received 30 minutes of progressive muscle relaxation (PMR) instructions per session for eight sessions. During the week following PMR, the subjects exercised for 30 minutes of continuous activity on the treadmill. The first and third 10 minutes of exercise were control periods. During the second 10 minutes (treatment period), the subjects elicited the relaxation response. Oxygen consumption and related measures were determined using the Beckman Metabolic Measurement Cart. A repeated measures analysis of variance (ANOVA) was used to analyze the data. During the treatment period, there were significant ($p<0.05$) decreases in frequency of breaths (Fb), expired ventilation (Ve), systolic blood pressure (SBP), and rate-pressure product (RPP) when compared to the two control periods. There were no significant ($p>0.05$) differences in Vt, oxygen consumption (VO_2), volume of carbon dioxide produced (VCO_2), respiratory exchange ratio (RER), and heart rate (HR). This study showed that the elicitation of the relaxation response during exercise did not decrease submaximal VO_2 and, therefore, did not alter running economy. Statistically significant changes in ventilation and blood pressure were associated with the elicitation of the relaxation response during exercise. Regarding the latter findings, there is ample evidence that a reduction in RPP has a positive and unequivocal beneficial influence on the work of the heart during exercise [2].

3. *Authors:* R. Robergs and L. Roberto

    Title: The Surprising History of the "HR max = 220-age" Equation

    Publication: *Journal of Exercise Physiologyonline* (Vol 5 No 2, 2002)

    Abstract: The estimation of maximal heart rate (HR max) has been a feature of exercise physiology and related applied sciences since the late 1930s. The estimation of HR max has been largely based on the formula; HR max = 220-age. This equation is often presented in textbooks without explanation or citation to original research. In addition, the formula and related concepts are included in most certification exams within sports medicine, exercise physiology, and fitness. Despite the acceptance of this formula, research spanning more than two decades reveals the large error inherent in the estimation of HR max (Sxy = 7-11 b/min). Ironically, inquiry into the history of this formula reveals that it was not developed from original research, but resulted from observation based on data from approximately 11 references consisting of published research or unpublished scientific compilations. Consequently, the formula HR max = 220-age has no scientific merit for use in exercise physiology and related fields. A brief review of alternate HR max prediction formula reveals that the majority of age-based univariate prediction equations also have large prediction errors (>10 b/min). Clearly, more research of HR max needs to be done using a multivariate model, and equations may need to be developed that are population (fitness, health status, age, exercise mode) specific.

4. *Authors:* E. Durak and L. Jennifer

    Title: Physical and Psychosocial Responses to Exercise in Cancer Patients: A Two-Year Follow-Up Survey with Prostate, Leukemia, and General Carcinoma.

    Publication: *Journal of Exercise Physiologyonline* (Vol 2 No 1, 1999)

    Abstract: Two years after the inception of the SBAC cancer exercise program, we report on the health status, physical function, and psychosocial benefits of cancer patients to a 20 week supervised exercise regime followed by self-reported exercise. The participants were categorized by cancer type in this program including: Prostate [Pr] (n=12), and Carcinoma/Leukemia [C/L] (n=13). Demographic information on these groups include: Age (yrs.): 71±7.3 [Pr], 44.6±17 [C/L], Cancer Stage: 2.0±.6 [Pr], 2.5±.7 [C/L], and years after diagnosis: 4.7+ 2.3 [Pr], 2.4± 2.5 [C/L]. Exercise lasted 20 weeks, and consisted of aerobic machines, progressive strength training, and specialty exercises. Participants completed a quality of life (QOL) survey after the exercise program. At two years, a follow-up survey on cancer status, health care information, and alternative health practices was solicited. Fitness results indicated changes in overall strength in both groups (+40% for Pr, +52% for C/L). Strength gains for the C/L group were significant (p=0.05). Time on aerobic machines also improved in both groups (+20% for Pr, +30% for C/L). Quality of life results indicated no perceived changes in 8 selected categories (ADLs, perceived fitness, and pain rating) for Pr, but significant changes in all categories for C/L groups. At two years, level of vigor (on a 10 point scale) was 8.5 for Pr and 9.0 for C/L. Vitamin supplementation was 77% for Pr and 84% for C/L. 92% of C/L group used alternative medicine (mostly meditation), but only 23% of Pr group used these modalities. One hundred percent of Pr group and 65% of C/L group continued to exercise at two-year follow-up. Compared to other cancer groups, there were no out-of-pocket medical expenses for either group. There was one recurrence of cancer and one reported death in the Pr group, none in the C/L group. Long-term participation in exercise may improve physical and psychological components in cancer recovery. Fitness and quality of life changes are more pronounced in C/L due in part to cancer stage, time after diagnosis, and severity of medical intervention before beginning exercise.

5. *Authors:* T. Boone and D. Diboll

Title: Physiologic Effects of a Standard Meal during Submaximal Exercise

Publication: New Zealand Journal of Sports Medicine (Vol 28 No 1, 2000)

Abstract: To investigate the physiologic effects of a meal during submaximal exercise, 14 healthy males exercised for 10 minutes at approximately 60% of age-predicted HR max. Each subject repeated the test protocol on two different mornings; one in which no food was consumed (control) and the other in which a 4186 kJ meal was consumed (treatment). The subjects were tested in randomized order. Measurements were performed with subjects in the fasting (9-hr) postabsorptive state. A significant ($p<0.05$) postprandial increase in heart rate (HR) and cardiac output (Q) were observed during submaximal exercise. Exercise systolic blood pressure (SBP), rate-pressure product (RPP = HR x SBP), estimated MVO_2, expired ventilation (Ve), tidal volume (Vt), and carbon dioxide production (VCO_2) were also significantly increased after the meal compared to fasting. These findings demonstrate that food results in significant physiological adjustments during exercise. In particular, the subjects' postprandial exercise VO_2 response was achieved by HR to increase Q. Similarly, there was a greater reliance upon Vt than the Fb response to increase Ve during the postprandial exercise condition.

6. *Authors:* T. Boone, S. Hansen, and A. Erlandson

Title: A. Cardiovascular Responses to Laughter: A Pilot Project

Publication: Applied Nursing Research (Vol 13 No 4, 2000)

Abstract: The purpose of this study was to determine cardiovascular responses to laughter. The CO_2 rebreathing method was used to determine cardiac output and understand the role of the central and peripheral components of oxygen consumption and its relation to energy expended. Eight college-age subjects participated in this study. During periods of 5 minutes each, while sitting in a comfortable chair, subjects first rested, then viewed a videotape of a well-known comedian, then remained sitting. A repeated-measures analysis of variance was used to analyze the data. During laughter, there were significant increases in stroke volume (SV) and cardiac output (Q) and significant decreases in artriovenous oxygen difference (a-vO_2 diff) and total peripheral resistance (SVR). Following laughter, there was a significant decrease in oxygen consumption (VO_2).

7. *Authors:* J. Janot, J. Steffen, J. Porcari, and M. Maher

Title: Heart Rate Responses and Perceived Exertion for Beginner and Recreational Sport Climbers during Indoor Climbing

Publication: Journal of Exercise Physiologyonline (Vol 3 No 1, 2000)

Abstract: The purpose of this investigation was to compare heart rate (HR) and ratings of perceived exertion (RPE) of beginner and recreational sport climbers during indoor climbing. Seventeen beginner (10 M and 7 F) and 17 recreational (10 M and 7 F) sport climbers climbed two routes that varied in difficulty (route 1 = 5.6, route 2 = 5.8 on the Yosemite Decimal Scale). HR responses were recorded at pre-climb, during climbing, and during recovery using a Polar XL HR monitor. RPE values were recorded after each climb using the Borg 15-point RPE scale. Significant differences ($p < .05$) in pre-climb HR, climbing HR, and RPE were found between beginner and recreational climbers, but not for recovery HR ($p > .05$). In addition, pre-climb HR responses were significantly higher ($p < .05$) than recovery HR in beginner climbers only. As expected, HR responses during climbing were significantly greater ($p < .05$) for route 2 compared to route 1 due to the increased difficulty of route 2. These results indicate that HR and RPE responses differ between beginner and recreational climbers during most conditions. The differences between the beginner and recreational climbers could be attributed to route familiarity, varied efficiency in climbing technique, a pressor response, or anxiety. These data show how climbers with varied skill levels respond during climbing and provide climbing instructors with information that may assist in designing climbing programs based on the individual skill of the climber.

8. *Authors:* R. Venkata, K. Surya, R. Sudhakar, and N. Balakrishna

Title: Effect of Changes in Body Composition Profile on VO_2 Max and Maximal Work Performance in Athletes

Publication: Journal of Exercise Physiologyonline (Vol 7 No 1, 2004)

Abstract: This study describes the changes in body composition profile and in turn the relationship to maximal work performance across three phases of athlete training. Ten national level male distance runners aged between 18 and 22 years from Sports Authority of Andhra Pradesh were studied during their transition (TP), Pre-competition (PP) and Competition (CP) phases of training. Body height, weight and circumferences were measured. Body composition was assessed by using skin-fold thickness at four sites. Physiological parameters such as VO_2 max (by means of indirect calorimetry) and maximal work performance (WR max) were estimated from treadmill running using the Bruce protocol. Quantification of training was done by the Time Allocation Pattern (TAP) and heart rate-work rate relationships. The results indicated a significant ($P<0.001$) increase in Lean Body mass (LBM) by 4.7%, VO_2 max (18%) and maximal work performance (WR max) by 37% from TP to CP. The change in training during this phase transition was 1.6 fold for intensity and 2 fold for duration. There were high significant correlations between LBM and VO_2 max, and WR max and VO_2 max. This study suggests that body composition is an important component in training-induced adaptations, and may influence physiological parameters resulting in an enhanced maximal work performance.

9. *Authors:* T. Boone and R. Cooper

Title: The Effects of Massage on Oxygen Consumption at Rest

Publication: American Journal of Chinese Medicine (Vol 28 No 1, 1995)

Abstract: This study determined the effect of massage on oxygen consumption at rest.   Ten healthy, adult males (mean age $=$ 28 years) volunteered to serve as subjects. During the Control Session, each subject was placed in the supine position on a massage table to remain motionless for 30 minutes. During the Treatment Session, each subject received a 30-minute sports massage of the lower extremities.   Oxygen consumption was determined via the Beckman Metabolic Measurement Cart, which was upgraded to estimate cardiac output using the CO_2 rebreathing (equilibrium) method. Paired t-tests were used for all tests of statistical significance. There was no significant difference in the subjects' oxygen consumption with the massage.   Also, there were no significant differences in heart rate, stroke volume, cardiac output, and tissue extraction during the massage.   These findings indicate: (1) that massaging the lower extremities result in neither an increase nor a decrease in the subjects' expenditure of energy at rest; and (2) that the energy cost of metabolism at rest is determined by the same central and/or peripheral adjustments.

10. *Authors:* M. Wattles and C. Harris

Title: The Relationship between Fitness Levels and Employee's Perceived Productivity, Job Satisfaction, and Absenteeism

Publication: Journal of Exercise Physiologyonline (Vol 6 No 1, 2003)

Abstract: This study examined the relationship between various components of health-related fitness and employees perceived productivity, job satisfaction and absenteeism.   One hundred forty-three employees of a northwest community completed a fitness assessment measuring percent body fat, cardiorespiratory endurance, flexibility, and muscular strength.   The participants were sent questionnaires to determine the relationship between fitness levels and perceived productivity and job satisfaction. Absenteeism rates, over a one-year period, were compared to the fitness level of each participant. Stepwise regression analyses using backward elimination were utilized to determine which health-related fitness components predicted productivity, job satisfaction and absenteeism. An alpha level of $p<0.05$ was used to determine statistical significance. Job satisfaction was influenced by the employees' level of cardiovascular endurance, with a beta weight of 0.28, $F\ (1,133) =10.90$, $p<0.001$, with less than 8% of variance in job satisfaction being explained by VO_2. Productivity was influenced by employees' level of muscular strength, with a beta weight of 0.21, $F\ (1,133) = 5.36$, $p<0.01$, with less than 8% of variance in productivity being explained by muscular strength level. This study found that higher levels of independent components of fitness may positively influence employees' productivity, job satisfaction and absenteeism.

11. *Author:* T. Boone

Title: Metabolic Cost of Walking With and Without a Shoe-Lift on the Contralateral Foot of an Immobilized Extended Knee

Publication: Australian Journal of Physiotherapy (Vol 47, 2001)

Abstract: The purpose of the present study was to determine the metabolic cost of walking with and without a shoe-lift on the contralateral foot of an immobilized knee. Eight male subjects were randomly allocated and participated in both the treatment (walking with a 2.5 cm shoe-lift) and control (walking without a shoe-lift) conditions. Cardiac output (Q) and related cardiovascular measurements were analyzed to determine the effect of a shoe-lift on central (heart rate, HR; stroke volume, SV) and peripheral (arteriovenous oxygen difference, a-vO_2 diff) components of oxygen consumption (VO_2). A metabolic analyzer was used to determine VO_2 (ml/kg/min), which was converted to oxygen cost (ml/kg/m). The shoe-lift had no significant (p>0.05) effect on VO_2 or oxygen cost. There were no significant differences in Q, HR, SV, a-vO₂ diff, systemic vascular resistance (SVR), carbon dioxide production (VCO_2), respiratory exchange ratio (RER), expired ventilation (Ve), tidal volume (Tv), and respiratory rate (Fb) between the two walking conditions with and without a shoe-lift. These findings demonstrate that a shoe-lift added to the contralateral foot of an immobilized extended knee does not produce clinically important effects on oxygen cost or efficiency during walking.

12. ***Authors:*** T. Boone, M. Tanner, and A. Radosevich

Title: Effects of a 10-Minute Back Rub on Cardiovascular Responses in Healthy Subjects

Publication: *American Journal of Chinese Medicine* (Vol 29 No 1, 2001)

Abstract: This study determined the cardiovascular responses to a 10-minute back rub. Twelve healthy, college-age males and females (mean age = 22 years) volunteered to participate as subjects. Using an ABA design, the subjects rested for 10 minutes (Control #1) on a padded plinth lying on one side. During the Treatment period, the back rub was administered, which was followed by Control #2. Oxygen consumption (VO_2) was determined via the Medical Graphics CPX/D metabolic analyzer, which also estimated cardiac output (Q) using the CO_2 rebreathing (equilibrium) method. A repeated measures ANOVA was performed to statistically compare the cardiovascular responses across the three periods. The back rub, when compared to Control #1, had no significant effect on VO_2, but the central and peripheral components were changed. Cardiac output was decreased as a result of the decreased stroke volume (SV), as a function of the increased peripheral resistance (PVR). We also found an increase in the extraction of oxygen (a-vO₂ diff) in the peripheral tissues. These results indicate that the VO_2 response during the back rub was achieved by reciprocal central (SV, Q) and peripheral (a-vO₂ diff) adjustments. Following the back rub, (i.e., Control #2 vs. Treatment), the decrease in VO_2, VCO_2, Ve, and a-vO_2 diff appears to indicate that it was effective in inducing relaxation. Since HR, SV, and Q were unchanged, the VO_2 response was a result of the decreased a-vO_2 diff. Hence, the findings suggest certain positive implications for the health care industry.

13. **Authors:** T. Boone, T. Westendorf, and P. Ayres

Title: Cardiovascular Responses to a Hot Tub Bath

Publication: *The Journal of Alternative and Complementary Medicine* (Vol 5 No 3, 1999)

Abstract: This study was conducted to determine the cardiovascular effects of 15 minutes of hot tub immersion at 39 degrees C. Five college-age subjects (4 males and 1 female) volunteered to participate in this study. Assessments were made while sitting first in a chair for 5 minutes and then in the hot tub for 15 minutes. Oxygen consumption (VO_2) and cardiac output (Q) measurements were made using a Medical Graphics CPX/D metabolic analyzer. Cardiac output was determined at minute 15 using the indirect CO_2 rebreathing procedure. The data were analyzed using the analysis of variance with repeated measures, which indicated that at minute 15, heart rate (HR) and Q were increased, which increased VO_2. The increase in Q was due to the HR response and the decrease in systemic vascular resistance (SVR). Mean arterial pressure (MAP) and systolic blood pressure (SBP) were decreased while double product (DP) was increased. There were no changes in SV or arteriovenous oxygen difference (a-vO_2 diff). These findings indicate that the HR and Q responses are necessary to the increase in metabolism (VO_2). Hot tub use within these time and temperature constraints should reduce concern over hot tub safety in college-age subjects.

14. *Author:* S. Blank

Title: Physiological Responses to Iyengar Yoga Performed by Trained Practitioners

Publication: Journal of Exercise Physiologyonline (Vol 9 No 1, 2006)

Abstract: The purpose of this study was to evaluate acute physiological responses to Hatha yoga asanas (poses) practiced in the Iyengar tradition. Preliminary data were collected on the impact of postural alignment on physiological responses. Intermediate/advanced level yoga practitioners (n=15 females) were monitored for heart rate (HR), oxygen uptake (VO_2), and brachial arterial blood pressure (n = 9) during a 90 min practice. The subjects, aged 43.5 ± 6.9 yr (average ± SD), had current weekly practice of 6.2 ± 2.4 hr/week and practice history 9.2 ± 7.2 yr. Physical characteristics of the subjects included: height (167.3 ± 4.1 cm), body mass (59.3 ± 7.2 kg), and percent body fat (23.1 ± 3.6 %). The practice included supine, seated, standing, inversions, and push up to back arch asanas maintained for 1-5 min. Physiological responses were significantly ($p < 0.05$) greater in standing asanas, inversions, and push up to back arch versus supine and seated asanas. The average metabolic equivalent (MET) of each pose did not exceed 5 METs. The practice expended 149.4 ± 50.7 Kcal. The cumulative time spent within a HR zone of 55-85% HR max was 29.7 ± 15.9 min (range = 10.8 – 59.9 min). Asana practice was classified as mild to moderate intensity exercise without evidence of a sustained cardiopulmonary stimulus. Intermediate and advanced practitioners maintained poses for up to 5 min without stimulating an undesirable pressor response. However, postural alignment significantly influenced blood pressure responses indicating that adherence to precise alignment has relevant physiological consequences for the yoga practitioner.

15. *Authors:* D. Redondo and T. Boone

Title: Central and Peripheral Circulatory Responses during Four Different Recovery Positions Immediately Following Submaximal Exercise

Publication: Journal of Exercise Physiologyonline (Vol 1 No 1, 1998)

Abstract: This study compared central and peripheral circulatory responses in 10 untrained males during the second minute of four different recovery positions. Prior to each recovery, subjects exercised at 75% heart rate (HR) intensity on the treadmill. The Beckman Metabolic Measurement Cart (MMC) and the CO_2 rebreathing procedure were used to measure oxygen consumption (VO_2) and cardiac output (Q), respectively. Analysis of variance (ANOVA) with repeated measures was followed by the Tukey's multiple comparison test to determine statistically significant differences among means ($p<0.05$). When compared to sitting, standing, and supine recoveries, the walking recovery resulted in significantly higher stroke volume (SV), VO_2, double product (DP), and estimated myocardial oxygen consumption (MVO_2). These data indicate that the walking recovery kept the subjects' cardiac effort elevated above the physiological responses of the passive recoveries. When compared to sitting and standing recoveries, the supine recovery demonstrated significantly higher SV and responses and significantly lower arteriovenous oxygen difference (a-vO_2 diff) and systemic vascular resistance (SVR) responses. However, since the VO_2, DP, and MVO_2 data were not significantly different during the three passive recoveries, the statistical decision is that the non-active recoveries are cardiovascularly similar. That is, whether the subject is sitting, standing, or in the supine position immediate post- exercise, the physiological responses are the same but only at 2 minutes of recovery [3].

16. *Authors:* G. Aldridge, J.S. Baker, and B. Davies

Title: Effects of Hydration Status on Aerobic Performance for a Group of Male University Rugby Players

Publication: Journal of Exercise Physiologyonline (Vol 8 No 5, 2005)

Abstract: The object of this study was to examine the effects of hydration status on exercise performance in a group of amateur athletes under conditions of hypohydration (HYPO) and euhydration (EUH) at 'neutrally stable' temperatures. Eight healthy, physically active, amateur University rugby players (age 21.0±1.4 yrs, BMI 28.3±6.1 kg/m^2) underwent two 12 hr programs of hydration (fluid abstinence and consumption at ~20 °C) in order to induce states of EUH and HYPO. The participants completed two 30 min cycle ergometer tests under each hydration state in a random order. Changes in performance were measured using heart rate (HR), rate of perceived exertion (RPE) and relative rate of oxygen uptake (VO$_2$). Urine osmolality values (UOsm) were also measured to quantify hydration status. UOsm values were EUH 385±184 mOsm/kg and HYPO 815±110 mOsm/kg. In the EUH condition, from rest to 30 min, HR values ranged from 78±12 to 116±12 beats/min, RPE 6±0 to 11±2 units and VO$_2$ 5.7±2.1 to 16.8±3.4 mL/kg/min. In the HYPO condition, HR increased from 85±9 to 124±13 beats/min, RPE 6±0 to 13±2 units, and VO$_2$ 6.2±2.8 to 20.1±3.5 ml/kg/min (mean±SD, $p \leq 0.05$). In conclusion, HR, RPE and VO$_2$ variables increased significantly under HYPO conditions when compared to EUH conditions at ~20°C and therefore having a detrimental effect on performance.

17. *Authors:* L.M. LeMura, S.P. von Dullivard, R. Carlonas, and J. Andreacci

Title: Can Exercise Training Improve Maximal Aerobic Power (VO$_2$ Max) in Children: A Meta-Analytic Review

Publication: Journal of Exercise Physiologyonline (Vol 2 No 3, 1999)

Abstract: This study was conducted to quantitatively examine the effects of physical training on maximal aerobic power (VO$_2$ max) in children using the meta-analytic technique. In addition, we examined the effects of experimental design, training protocol, gender, age, and testing procedures on the VO_2 max of children. Past research used in the analyses were delimited to studies examining the effects of various forms of muscular strength and endurance training in children <13 years, resulting in a total of 91 studies. However, as numerous studies failed to provide sufficient information or adequate statistics, the final pool of research was confined to 20 studies with 32 effect sizes (ES), totaling 562 subjects. Studies which utilized a control group generated a mean pre-post training ES of 1.1±0.1, compared to a mean ES of 0.32±0.2 from those in which subjects served as their own controls ($p<0.0009$). Studies that were cross sectional (XS) typically reported a higher VO_2 max in the trained group (ES = 1.7±0.3) compared to pre-to-post test designs (ES = 0.63±0.6). Analyses of the subjects characteristics indicated that children in the 8 to 10 year old (ES = 0.47±0.4) range were trainable; however not nearly to the same extent as their 11 to 13 year old counterparts (ES = 1.1±0.7, $p<0.02$). The mean ES for girls and boys was 1.0±0.6 and 0.64±0.9, respectively. An analysis of investigations which utilized a sufficiently intense training stimulus, vs. an inadequate training stimulus, resulted in significant improvements in VO_2 max after training (ES = 0.33±0.2 vs. ES = 1.2±0.5, $p<0.0004$). Children improved their VO_2 max by an average of 6.0% (47.1±4.3 versus 50.1±4.6) after training. The results of this quantitative review indicate that children are indeed trainable, but the changes in VO_2 max are modest and are significantly impacted by the experimental design of the investigation, the age of the children, and the nature of training stimulus.

132

18. *Author:* T.A. Astorino

Title: Examination of Running Economy and Run Performance in Collegiate Cross-Country Athletes

Publication: Journal of Exercise Physiologyonline (Vol 9 No 2, 2006)

Abstract: The present study was undertaken to test multiple measures of running performance in college runners. Prior to the season, nine men and seven women (mean age, VO_2 max, and maximal heart rate = 19.6 ± 1.5 yr, 61.8 ± 8.8 mL/kg/min, and 196.4 ± 7.2 b/min, respectively) competitive in Division NAIA cross-country participated in the study. In a single 1-hour session, body composition (sum of 3 skin folds), RE (treadmill running at sub-threshold speed with constant heart rate and RER < 1.0), and VO_2 max/anaerobic threshold were assessed. During exercise, heart rate and gas exchange data were continuously obtained. The ventilatory threshold was obtained from plots of gas exchange measures (V_E and/or VCO_2) versus heart rate (HR). VO_2max in women was equal to 53.7 ± 2.6 mL/kg/min, and 69.1 ± 3.6 mL/kg/min, respectively, in men. At speeds ranging from 6.0 – 7.7 mph, RE in women ranged from 29.9 – 39.7 mL/kg/min; whereas in men running at speeds from 7.5 – 9.2 mph, RE was equal to 37.8 – 46.1 mL/kg/min. There was a significant correlation between RE at the highest speed and VO_2 max (r = 0.90, $p<0.01$) and run time (r = 0.62, $p<0.05$). Linear regression of the relationship between RE and speed yielded the following equation, $y = 5.62x - 4.37$, $r^2 = 0.86$. No differences ($p>0.05$) in slope and y-intercept for the regression equations were noted between women ($y = 4.44x + 3.51$, $r^2 = 0.51$) and men ($y = 5.08x + 0.40$, $r^2 = 0.58$). The data indicate; 1) a strong relationship between submaximal VO_2 (RE) and VO_2 max, 2) no gender differences in the relationship between running speed and RE, and 3) VO_2 max is a significant predictor of RE.

19. **Authors:** C. Marra, M. Bottaro, R. J. Oliveira, and J. S. Novaes

Title: Effect of Moderate and High Intensity Aerobic Exercise on the Body Composition of Overweight Men

Publication: *Journal of Exercise Physiologyonline* (Vol 8 No 2, 2005)

Abstract: The optimal aerobic exercise training intensity to improve body composition in overweight men is unclear. The purpose of this study was to determine the effect of 14 weeks of high intensity versus moderate intensity aerobic exercise of equal work output on body composition in overweight men (BMI = 25-29.9 kg/m^2). Sixteen sedentary military men (18 - 33 yrs) were randomized in two equal groups (n=8): 1) moderate intensity exercise (MI; 60 - 70% of their maximum heart rate; HR max), and 2) high intensity exercise (HI; 75 - 90% HR max). The aerobic exercise (jogging/running) training program was performed three days/wk. Relative body fat (% BF) was assessed by dual energy x-ray absorptiometry (DXA) (Lunar DPX - IQ). Significant differences between and within the groups were analyzed using a two-way split-plot analysis of variance (SPANOVA). Statistical significance was accepted at $p<0.05$. After the 14 wks of the aerobic exercise program the mean %BF of the HI significantly ($p<0.05$) decreased to 22.49 % (Δ=4.91%). The decrease in mean %BF (Δ=1.4 %) in the MI was not significant ($p>0.05$). It is concluded that 14 wks of HI aerobic exercise may be more effective in improving body composition than MI aerobic exercise in overweight young military men with physical characteristics similar to the present study.

20. **Authors:** C.D. Ashley, P.D. Reneau, J.P. Roy, and P.A. Bishop

Title: Effects of a Short, Submaximal Run at Different Times of Day on Heat Strain

Publication: *Journal of Exercise Physiologyonline* (Vol 9 No 1, 2006)

Abstract: In hot weather, radiant heat and dry-bulb temperatures are lowest and humidity is highest early and late in the day. The purpose of this study was to determine heat stress responses of running at different times of day.

Moderately trained male runners (n=10) performed three 4.84 kilometer runs in the morning, noon and in the evening at a self-selected pace in a hot climate. The wet-bulb globe temperature (WBGT) was used to evaluate environmental conditions. Heart rate and rectal temperature was recorded before and after each exercise bout. The dry bulb and wet bulb temperatures were lower and humidity was higher during the morning runs ($p<0.05$). Running times, heart rates and rectal temperatures were not different among the trials ($p>0.05$). In our experienced runners, heat stress responses to a short, submaximal run were equivalent in the morning, noon and evening. Assuming an early-morning or late afternoon run obviates heat injury concerns seems unwise. However, it appears that acclimation may serve to enhance heat dissipation mechanisms and reduce heat strain.

Chapter Twelve

Accredited Exercise Physiology Programs

Now, more than ever, ethical thinking is critical to the credibility of exercise physiology. While it is almost a cliché to make such a statement, the fact is this: Exercise physiologists have not addressed ethics within mainstream academic agendas.

The *American Society of Exercise Physiologists* was founded in 1997 to unite exercise physiologists and to promote the professional development of exercise physiology. The Society promotes exercise physiologists by: (a) enhancing the recognition of their work and educating the public about their importance and functions in the athletic, fitness, allied health and medical fields; and (b) fostering the exchange of ideas and research among exercise physiologists and the public sector through the Internet and national meetings.

Among the goals and objectives of ASEP is the continued development and refinement of the Standards of Professional Practice [1], which are linked to the ASEP Code of Ethics, the "Exercise Physiologist Certified" (EPC) exam, and a nationwide accreditation program. While certification evaluates the competence of the individual exercise physiologist, accreditation process is a system for ensuring that the academic programs preparing students for the exercise physiology profession are of a high quality.

Work began on the development of the accreditation program in early 1998. The accreditation document [2] itself was submitted for final approval by the ASEP Board of Directors at the 1999 national meeting. The manual represents the first-ever work by exercise physiologists to identified minimal standards that are acceptable for educating students in exercise physiology.

Academic accreditation is an important and essential component to any profession. The Board of Accreditation is interested in working with the administrators and faculty of academic programs to ensure that the ASEP standards are met and that the graduating students are worthy of the professional title – "Exercise Physiologist." The benefits from result from accreditation include:

- Academic programs are critically evaluated and improved,
- Students are better prepared for certification exams and the workforce,
- Employers are confident that they are hiring competent professionals, and
- Students gravitate to ASEP-accredited programs, as there is little incentive to enroll in an academic institution that is not recognized by ASEP.

At the present time, the Board of Accreditation within *The Center for Exercise Physiology-online* has determined that the following academic institutions meet accreditation standards [3]:

- Slippery Rock University – [http://www.sru.edu/]
- University of New Mexico - Albuquerque – [http://www.unm.edu/]
- Marquette University – [http://www.marquette.edu/]
- Bloomsburg University - [http://www.bloomu.edu/index.php]
- The College of St. Scholastica - [http://www.css.edu/]

Slippery Rock University of Pennsylvania

The SRU Exercise Science program is the *first* in the United States to be accredited by the *American Society of Exercise Physiologists*. The program has many hands-on learning experiences with a variety of populations with well-qualified, caring, and knowledgeable student-oriented faculty. The course work is supported by state of the art laboratory facilities and student-faculty research opportunities

Mission Statement

The purpose of the Exercise Science Program at Slippery Rock University is to develop competent and contributing entry-level professionals in the field of exercise science by providing quality academic preparation that incorporates both classroom and supervised practical experiences.

Program Outcomes

Professional Interaction and Communication

- To interact and communicate effectively by presenting information in oral, written, and technology formats; collaborating with professionals and peers; expressing ideas clearly; and giving and receiving feedback.

Professional Competence

- To utilize knowledge, skills, and abilities to evaluate health behavior and risk factors; develop, implement, and evaluate exercise programs, and employ self-help strategies to motivate individuals to adopt and maintain positive lifestyle behaviors.

Professional Ethics and Conduct

- To demonstrate behavior that is consistent with professional standards of practice.

Personal and Professional Development

- To continuously improve knowledge, skills, and abilities and to uphold a professional image through actions and appearance.

Professional Decision Making (Problem Solving)

- To demonstrate critical thinking by making decisions based on multiple perspectives and evidence-based practice.

Note: The Exercise Science major will become the Exercise Physiology major by the end of the 5th year of accreditation, which is true for all other accredited programs that are not exercise physiology majors to begin with.

The academic major is designed to prepare students to serve as exercise physiologists in a variety of physical fitness and/or health promotion programs. The theoretical coursework is concentrated in the areas of exercise physiology, physical fitness assessment, and fitness and wellness programming. These courses are supplemented by foundation courses selected from the natural and behavioral sciences.

Practical application and experience is provided through fieldwork at the Russell Wright Fitness Center, located on the campus of Slippery Rock University. The culminating experience is a full-time (12-credit) internship in one of approximately 75 quality programs, which have cooperative agreements with the university. The internship sites are selected through careful advisement to provide the best possible experiences for students in either corporate, hospital, commercial or community settings.

Requirements for the Major

A. **Required Courses**

(1) **Exercise Science Core Courses - Credits: 21**

- *Introduction to Exercise Science*: An introductory level class for exercise science majors in which the student will trace the origin of the profession and be given the opportunity to identify professional characteristics through observation and interaction with professionals in the field. The class will encompass career planning, internship opportunities, and current research that pervades the profession.

- *Applied Anatomy Credits:* A study of the structure of the human body with particular emphasis upon the skeletal, muscular, nervous and cardiovascular systems as related to scientifically sound and practical exercise programs.

- *Measurement and Statistical in Exercise Science:* Focuses on measurement, data collection, and statistical treatment (descriptive and inferential) of health and fitness data associated with exercise science.

140

- *Biomechanics:* Analysis of human motion based on anatomic, physiologic and mechanical principles.

- *Exercise Physiology I:* Study of the physiological bases of exercise with emphasis on the responses and adaptations of the systems of the body to a variety of exercise stimuli. Exercise physiology principles are studied by means of participation in weekly laboratory experiences.

- *Exercise Leadership (Group Fitness):* This course is designed to provide specialized instruction and opportunities for practical application in the following areas of group fitness activities: hi/lo impact, step, slide, water aerobics, resistance training, funk/hip-hop, cardio kick box, interval and circuit training. Each topic will be covered in detail with respect to physiological and biomechanical principles, choreography, safety, and modifications for participation of special populations. Current trends and research in the area of group fitness instruction will be explored.

- *Exercise Leadership (Strength Fitness):* Designed to provide both the theoretical and practical knowledge to effectively design, organize and conduct strength fitness programs. Specific emphasis will be placed on the physiological and kinesiological principles, training guidelines and safety procedures in developing and administering programs for general strength fitness, competitive weightlifting and bodybuilding.

(2) Specialization Area Courses

- *Exercise Science Internship:* This course is designed to provide students an opportunity to apply Exercise Science career-oriented skills in a supervised work experience in a university approved fitness, wellness or rehabilitative agency.

141

- *Physical Fitness Assessment:* Provides the theoretical and practical basis to select and utilize properly the instrumentation and techniques for physical fitness assessment.

- *Exercise Physiology II:* This is a laboratory-based course that focuses on cardiovascular and respiratory responses and adaptations to a variety of exercise stimuli in both healthy individuals and those with various cardiopulmonary diseases. Special emphasis will be placed upon electrocardiogram monitoring and interpretation, graded exercise testing, and the influence of various environmental factors upon cardiac and pulmonary function.

- *Exercise Prescription:* This course provides the theoretical knowledge base to design safe and effective personalized exercise programs for various populations. Emphasis is placed on prescribing individualized cardiovascular, musculoskeletal and weight control programs for the apparently healthy, the chronically diseased, the elderly, children and pregnant females.

- *Exercise Science (Senior Synthesis):* Designed to provide students with experiences which allow them to apply their knowledge and skills in a practical worksite situation.

- *Worksite Wellness Promotion:* This course is designed to provide current information in the area of wellness and health promotion in various workplace settings. An overview of various concepts and issues relating to worksite wellness programs will be discussed. Guidelines for planning, implementing, and evaluating successful programs will be analyzed.

- *Nutrition and Exercise:* Focuses on the specific nutritional requirement for physical conditioning for persons involved in competitive and recreational activities. Emphasizes the development and maintenance of a healthy cardiovascular system.

The Exercise Science Program at the undergraduate level has a multidisciplinary and interdisciplinary knowledge base and is designed to enable practitioners to bridge the gap between theory, research, and practice. This program prepares undergraduates to be exercise scientists for health and fitness clubs, corporate health programs, and clinical rehabilitation settings. It offers 22 courses in exercise physiology.

The mission of the Exercise Science Program is to promote physical activity and exercise as a means to attain and maintain health, physical fitness, and quality of life throughout the lifespan. The faculty strives to develop model programs that integrate theory, research and clinical practice and exemplify quality teaching and learning for exercise science professionals and the public at-large.

The Exercise Physiology Laboratories are well-equipped to cover such testing specialties as body composition, exercise testing, indirect calorimetry, pulmonary function, cardiovascular function, blood and muscle biochemistry, altitude physiology, hyperbaric physiology, microgravity, muscular strength, exercise equipment validation, and sports physiology.

Special Faculty Highlight: A Professional Philosophy

> *Professor Robert A. Robergs, PhD, FASEP, EPC*
> *Director, Center for Exercise and Human Physiology*
> *The University of New Mexico – Albuquerque, NM*

I think it is important to know how a person in the exercise sciences views his or her job, and the related professional functions and responsibilities. This is especially important in the field of the exercise sciences, as we are not viewed as professionals, nor function as professionals in the strict sense of the word "professional." For example, in the context of vocational employment, the word profession implies that there is some sort of organized body that oversees the duties and conduct of the members of the profession. Unlike most dictionary definitions of the word "profession," to be a professional involves more than earning an income and livelihood from the employment. A profession has a template of standards and ethics from which members of the profession must adhere. These requirements must be developed, policed, and enforced by the members of the profession, thereby upholding another quality of professional existence, self regulation.

As a university-based exercise physiologist, who directs my functions? Is there any external body that overseas how faculty function in exercise physiology within their discipline? What is my code of ethics? How can my functions be fairly evaluated if there are no standards, devised by exercise physiologists, for my peers to read, understand, and implement in their evaluation of me? What does all this mean to the quality of the work that I do and, more importantly, to the consistency of the standards of this quality between the different exercise physiology programs throughout the United States?

My identification of the aforementioned questions have led me to be convinced that exercise physiology is an advanced and admirable topic of academic and research inquiry. As you may or may not know, I have pursued this belief by focusing considerable time and energy by co-founding a professional organization for exercise physiologists in 1997 (the *American Society of Exercise Physiologists*, ASEP), presiding over this organization (1998-2000), and accepting the responsibilities of editor-in-chief of the ASEP Internet-based research journal (JEPonline; April 1998 to the present).

A person with an undergraduate degree in exercise science/physiology is highly trained, at least equal to any other recognized allied health profession such as nursing, physical therapy, nutrition, and dietetics. In fact, exercise science students undergo more training than many other medical-related professions (e.g., pulmonary therapists and radiology technicians.). Consequently, exercise science students who major in exercise physiology deserve to graduate and be recognized as a professional. After all, the body of knowledge and laboratory skills taught in exercise physiology is needed in corporate fitness, health and wellness, community fitness, and clinical markets. There is also tremendous potential for entrepreneurial applications of this body of knowledge.

Teaching

As a university professor, teaching is my primary responsibility. I am a university-based educator because I believe that teaching is perhaps the most satisfying and important vocation of them all. To teach has been a desire of mine since my high school studies, and has continued to grow in importance to me during my undergraduate training as a physical educator, my 3 years of high school teaching in Australia, my 6 years of graduate education and training, and my continuous employment as a university teacher since 1990.

However, I did not always recognize that teaching was so important to my professional existence and clear conscience. When I started my university employment, I viewed the undergraduate students as the reason for why I can be there. I viewed the graduate students as cheap labor to assist me in my research, and I was the center of my professional functions. **I was a professor to develop my career and not the careers of my students**. I wanted to complete "x" number of research projects each year, submit and present "x" number of research abstracts each year at scientific meetings, and feed my ego as often as I could by seeing my name in print in a prestigious research journal. Recognition as a researcher was to be my stamp of success, and teaching was just a means to that end in the university arena.

After approximately 5 years of this existence, it became very clear to me that the development of my career was not the purpose for my being a university professor. The students deserved to be the focus of my professional existence, and although being a productive researcher had a positive impact on my competencies as a teacher, my research moved from being the end objective, to the means to being a better teacher.

145

I strongly believe that teaching is more than a classroom activity. In fact, university-based employment also recognizes this, as duties such a advising, mentoring, directing theses and dissertations, and curriculum development are all components of the "teaching" component of tenure. I receive tremendous satisfaction and, at the same time, recognize the power and responsibility given to me, in directing the professional future of my students. Whether these students are at the undergraduate or the PhD level, I have the power to develop their outlook on life and shape a path for them so that they can reach their professional aspirations. The satisfaction from teaching is not confined to the grade sheet, but has an arguably greater test in the employability of the students, and the eventual employment of the students in a field where they can use their exercise physiology training.

My transformation from a self-centered ego driven academic to a student and teaching oriented professional was first expressed in my desire to write (co-author) my own exercise physiology textbook. I wanted to improve the teaching standards within exercise physiology, and a new book seemed a great, although time consuming and tedious, place to start. I co-authored my first book, which is entitled: *Exercise Physiology: Exercise, Performance and Clinical Applications* in 1996. It is a graduate and advanced level exercise physiology text. I have co-authored two other books, they are: *Clinical Exercise Physiology*, which was published in 1994 and *Fundamental Principles of Exercise Physiology: For Fitness, Performance and Health* in 2000.

My evaluation of the exercise sciences in the United States also led me to believe that too many university-based exercise physiologists still function as I did when I began my career. How could I think otherwise? Exercise physiology was a discipline that was drifting along with no direction, and each year was being devoured, topic by topic, by other professions. There was no organization that existed to nurture exercise physiology and, as I found out, no sports medicine organization that recognized these needs to be important.

146

Why did my predecessors not nurture the very discipline they helped develop? This question still irritates my soul, yet rather than accept this situation, I wanted to change it for the good of the education of the students in exercise physiology, and the improvement of their eventual employment conditions. Consequently, the co-founding of ASEP was just as much an issue of my recognition to the importance of the educational processes in exercise science, as it was a means to allow communication at all levels and on all topics by exercise physiologists.

Research

When reading research on issues pertinent to exercise physiology there are some glaring inadequacies. Exercise scientists, as well as medical and pure and applied scientists too often use inadequate numbers of subjects, ignore limitations to statistical power and the related existence of type II errors, and are over-reliant on research designs suited solely to t-tests and analysis of variance techniques. Similarly, research studies are designed to control for as many extraneous variables as possible, making it more likely to find a significant influence of the dependent variable, while at the same time limiting the application of the findings to the real world.

Based on the previous information, a main line of inquiry within the exercise research is to determine physiological differences in one dependent variable between groups (cross-sectional), or between controlled conditions (experimental) using one (repeated measures) or more groups. As previously explained, many variables are controlled, and there is an underlying assumption that one variable is most important in determining the physiological responses to whatever is the controlled or differentiating variable(s) at question. This single variable becomes the dependent variable, and efforts are made to reveal how influential it is in exercise physiology.

Most exercise scientists and research scientists in general are taught to follow this line of reasoning, and the statistical and research design requirements

147

of this approach. However, I have recently come to question this approach. Why should we expect to find one singularly important variable in any physiological system, when it is clear from human physiology, biochemistry, and molecular biology that the body is regulated by many inter-related phenomena? For example, when one regulation system is made redundant another takes over, and often a regulation system is dependent on the physiological interaction of multiple variables. For a good example of this fact, see my 1998 manuscript on the multiple determinants to VO_2 max during acute hypobaric hypoxia.

In my opinion, we would learn more from human physiology research if we used more subjects in a given research study, and then used this approach to investigate the influence of multiple variables on the physiology at question. Surely results that showed the relative importance of multiple variables to a physiological response provide more information and improves understanding better than the isolation of one variable under highly constrained/controlled conditions.

My future philosophy to research is to therefore use larger sample sizes (>24) in all the research that I do. I want to exploit the added statistical power of using multiple regression, multiple analysis of variance, and even more advanced approaches such as modeling, time series designs, and path analyses. In addition, because of the limitations in past research that has used small sample sizes (<8) and is likely to have caused type II errors, there is a body of research that is fundamental to the core of exercise physiology content that needs to be redone with my proposed improvements in research design, and the increased sensitivity of today's computerized technologies. Examples of these fundamental topics are:

- What are the heart rate, stroke volume, and cardiac output response to incremental exercise?
- What are the heart rate, stroke volume, and cardiac output response to incremental exercise during acute hypoxia?
- What are the criteria used in the assessment and verification of VO_2 max?

- What are the endocrine influences during exercise (acute) and in response to training (chronic)?
- What are the acid-base changes during different exercise conditions, as well as the recovery from acidosis?
- What are the gender differences in the metabolic response to exercise?

Service

My philosophy to the service component of my university tenure has evolved with my increasing years of university employment. Obviously, service duties must be curtailed in the early years of university pre-tenure existence so that efforts can be focused on teaching and research, the two most important components of the tenure and promotion evaluation process. Nevertheless, junior faculty in a university setting must become involved in service, especially at their college level, to make themselves recognized by peer faculty from other academic programs. Placing a face and personality to a name on a folder is too important for words to describe during any evaluation process.

Once tenured, the balance of service with the other duties of teaching and research depends on the individual. Some people are more suited to service on committees than others, just as some people are better teachers and researchers. Personally, I am so involved in graduate education that my teaching and research take priority over service. I am responsible for the education and professional development of too many students to spend large amounts of time and energy in university service. My graduate student load drains my time due to the added requirements to procure grant money for our (mine and my students') research, and the time to train my students and assist in pilot research for their eventual thesis and dissertation research.

In addition to service to the university and local community, there is also service to your profession. Since 1997, I have devoted al large amount of time and energy into the *American Society of Exercise Physiologists* (ASEP), presiding over this organization, organizing national meetings. The time and effort I have devoted to this need has been considerable. This is a commitment that I view to be important as it not only improves exercise physiology as a discipline and profession, but also improves the future employment and professional recognition of the very students that I am educating and training.

In recent years, my involvement in ASEP, and the increasing international recognition these functions have directed to me, have also improved the employability of my students. This is a very satisfying result of service to a profession, and I am hopeful that many more exercise physiologists will eventually come to recognize the positive feedback that results from performing service to their own discipline and profession [4].

Marquette University

A Major in Exercise Science

With personal health and fitness occupying much of our nation's attention, a major in exercise science (where students get to study anatomy, kinesiology, physiology, nutrition and exercise) is an excellent way to tap into a plentiful job market to promote a healthier nation through exercise and wellness programs. A degree in exercise science opens the door to professional opportunities in fitness training. It is also a great launching pad for students who want to go into sports medicine, physical therapy, athletic training, occupational therapy, and advanced exercise physiology.

Typical Exercise Science Program
Freshman Year
- Rhetoric and Composition
- Rhetoric and Composition
- General Chemistry
- Culture and Health

- Emergency Care
- General Chemistry
- Introduction to Exercise Science
- Anatomy and Physiology
- Introduction to Theology
- Surface Anatomy
- General Biology

Sophomore Year
- Biochemistry and Physiology
- Theory of Ethics
- Introduction to Psychology
- Motor Learning
- Philosophy of Human Nature
- Kinesiology
- Psychology of Measurements and Statistics
- General Biology

Junior Year
- Exercise Leadership
- Exercise Testing, Prescription and ECG
- Strength and Conditioning
- Elective
- Practicum I
- Nutrition and Exercise
- Nutrition and Health
- Electives

Senior Year
- Medical Ethics
- Exercise Program Management

- Exercise for Special Populations
- Advanced Exercise Physiology
- Electives

Bloomsburg University

Mission Statement

The Department of Exercise Science and Athletics embraces the concept that wellness and the quality of life of all persons is enhanced by participation in physical activity and sport. The department focuses primarily on incorporating the scientific basis of human performance into careers in exercise science and related health settings. The objective the faculty is to stay abreast of innovative educational opportunities via scholarship, research, practical learning experiences, and technological applications. Students are empowered to critically evaluate the challenges associated with living in modern society through inquiry, critical thinking, communication, and responsible self-expression.

About the Department

The academic major is designed to prepare students for the wide range of careers in the growing field of wellness and fitness, Exercise Science at Bloomsburg is unique among State System of Higher Education universities. This challenging and demanding program leads to careers in education, corporate wellness programs, cardiac rehabilitation, health care, sports medicine, and research environments. Emphasis is on the interpreted aspects of wellness and fitness, gerontology, nutrition, stress management, alternative medicine and therapies, and cardiac rehabilitation in a rapidly evolving professional field.

Major national corporations and graduate programs actively recruit Bloomsburg students. Many large companies, concerned with the health and

152

productivity of employees, seek exercise physiology professionals to develop and manage corporate wellness facilities; other graduates go on to establish their own businesses in the personal training and fitness field or into sports medicine. A number of leading universities, including Bloomsburg, offer graduate study in Exercise Science and Adult Fitness involving clinical and research internships to encompass the full spectrum of health, including cardiac rehabilitation, physiological assessment and training for optimal performance. Student factors that suggest a high probability of success include strong interpersonal skills, an intense desire to help others, versatility in individual skill and fitness abilities, and strength in sciences, particularly those related to anatomy and physiology. The faculty offer advisement to assist individual students in tailoring a specific program of study to prepare them for career objectives.

Exercise Science

In addition to general education requirements (54 semester hours), a minimum of 42 semester hours are required for the academic major, with the remaining 18 required credits for area of concentration.

A. Required Courses

- Introduction to Exercise Science
- First Aid, Safety, AED
- Anatomy and Physiology I
- Anatomy and Physiology II
- Kinesiology
- Exercise Physiology I
- Introduction to Nutrition
- Research Methods in Exercise Science
- ECG Interpretation/Exercise Testing
- Exercise Prescription/Program
- Exercise Physiology II

- Exercise and You
- Human Sexuality or Alcohol Use and Abuse

Concentration courses within the Department include:
- Current Issues in Health Promotion
- Prevention of Athletic Injuries
- Hiking and Backpacking
- Outdoor Life
- Resistance Training Techniques
- Group Fitness Instructor
- Resistance Training
- Aquatic fitness Programming
- Psychology of Sport
- Exercise and Mental Health
- Decisions for Healthy Behavior
- Introduction to Coaching
- Recreation Education
- School Camping/Outdoor Education
- Women in Sport
- Sport Nutrition
- Adult Health and Development
- Current Issues in Sport and Exercise
- Exercise Prescription and Programming for Special Populations
- Cardiac Rehabilitation
- Exercise Specialist and Health Fitness Instructor
- Clinical Exercise Physiology

The College of St. Scholastica

Overview

Exercise physiology is the comprehensive delivery of professional services concerned with the analysis, improvement, and maintenance of health and fitness, rehabilitation of heart disease and other chronic diseases and/or disabilities, and the guidance and counsel of athletes and others interested in athletics, sports training, and human adaptability to acute and chronic exercise. Academic preparation offers a unique and comprehensive study of human stress, physical activity, and lifestyle issues. Results from exercise physiology research studies help to discern the psycho-physiological effects of exercise, and the extent to which regular exercise helps in developing and maintaining cardiovascular and musculoskeletal integrity.

Exercise Physiology at St. Scholastica

The Department of Exercise Physiology offers a Bachelor of Arts degree in Exercise Physiology. Exercise physiologists are prepared for careers in the management of health related risk factors, fitness and athletic development, and cardiopulmonary programs to rehabilitate patients with heart and/or lung disease, and careers in research in the above-mentioned areas of healthcare.

If you are looking for a career with the potential for advancement as a healthcare professional, there are great opportunities as an exercise physiologist. Students who graduate from St. Scholastica are encouraged to sit for the "Exercise Physiologist Certification" exam. Many are board certified exercise physiologists who work in professional sports, fitness industry, clinical settings, research, pharmacology, the military, and government research. Still other students have been accepted into exercise physiology graduate programs and/or other healthcare areas of study (e.g., physical therapy, medical school, and nursing).

Course Sequence

Junior Year

- *Sports Nutrition:* Emphasis is on the role of a sound diet in sports and athletic programs with special attention paid to the ethics of athletics and the negative impact of sports supplements on athletes and society.

- *Psychophysiology Stress and Exercise:* This course examines the psychological and physiological dimensions of the stress response at rest and during exercise. Attention is given to a critical consideration of lifestyle factors and the extent to which society at large is responsible for (or victimized by) disease. Various stress reduction techniques (such as progressive muscular relaxation techniques) will be practiced and physiologically evaluated using the metabolic analyzers in the exercise physiology laboratory.

- **Kinesiology:** This course consists of a study of the origin, insertion, and function of the major muscles of the upper and lower extremities. Emphasis is also placed on the nerves throughout the body, including but not limited to, the brachial plexus and the lumbosacral plexus, the sliding filament theory of muscle contraction, and the functional analysis of weight lifting, flexibility, and athletic activities.

- *Exercise Physiology:* Emphasis is placed on the cardiovascular physiology of the body at rest and during exercise, the management of lifestyle risk factors related to heart disease and other dysfunctions that associate with sedentary living. The role of different submaximal and maximal ergometric test protocols used in exercise physiology laboratories are covered.

- *Physiological Assessment:* Emphasis is on basic to advanced instrumentation used to evaluate flexibility, body composition, muscular strength and endurance, as well as exercise test protocols used to evaluate individuals ranging from the elite athlete to middle-aged and elderly adults. Application of various stress test protocols and exercise programs

156

with individualized exercise prescriptions for both healthy and diseased individuals. Emphasis is on progression, safety and legal ramifications of exercise as a therapeutic intervention.

- *Cardiac Rehabilitation:* This course examines the multi-disciplinary factors considered responsible for coronary artery disease. Administrative, financial and program development decisions, stress test protocols, exercise principles and legal concerns, and common psychosocial issues and concerns are covered as they relate to the post-myocardial infarction and pulmonary patients.
- *Biomechanics:* Emphasis is on fundamental principles, calculations and applications of biomechanical analysis to the human body at rest and during movement. Attention is given to the relationship of biomechanics to kinesiology and exercise physiology in order to understand the role of physical stressors as they influence significant clinical changes in the body.
- *Statistics:* Emphasis is placed on research design, data collection, and statistical analysis (e.g., t-tests, analysis of variance, correlation, etc) including manuscript development and publishing.

Senior Year

- *Exercise Electrocardiography:* Students read electrocardiograms of subjects at rest and during exercise. They will also read and evaluate the electrocardiograms of post-myocardial infarction patients in cardiac rehabilitation programs. Emphasis is also placed on exercise prescription, cardiac medications, emergency procedures, code of ethics, standards of practice, and legal issues associated with the clinical setting and exercise physiology.
- *Advanced Exercise Physiology:* This course examines the human cardiovascular response at rest and during exercise, as well as to various stressors. Applications and calculations include acute central, peripheral

157

and metabolic adjustments and adaptations to biophysiological stressors. Students are required to demonstrate a thorough understanding of the cardiovascular calculations both in class and in the laboratory.

- *Exercise Physiology Research I:* This course presents the experimental designs and data analysis procedures used to conduct and report scientific research. Emphasis is on correctly reading and interpreting scientific articles, and on the student's ability to substantiate research discussions with hands-on research activities in the laboratory.

- *Internship (16 credits):* A supervised off-campus internship that allows the student to apply theoretical knowledge and hands-on laboratory skills to "real life" situations.

  or

- *Research Courses*
  - o *Advanced Lab Research:* Emphasizes student use of exercise physiology instrumentation to study currently important laboratory techniques. Special attention is given to the analysis of the exponential and equilibrium methods for determining cardiac output and its relationship to oxygen consumption. The student's ability to plan for and engage in an intensive laboratory study of a specific research problem is also important in this course.

  - o *Seminar in Exercise Physiology:* Centers on the presentations of exercise physiology topics by students and faculty. The course examines the specificity of professional development, exercise physiology as a profession, exercise physiology professional organizations, certification, licensure and accreditation.

  - o *Exercise Physiology Research II:* Focuses on the ethics of scientific research, data reduction, writing, and publishing in exercise physiology. This course also examines issues of scientific fraud, "publish or perish," plagiarism, critiquing research studies and accuracy of references. The student will be expected to propose and independently carry out a research project, reduce the data, develop a research manuscript, and produce a document consistent with the published format of a specific exercise physiology journal.

o *Exercise Immunology:* This course addresses the relationship between exercise and susceptibility to illness, particularly with reference to the mechanisms responsible for exercise-induced changes in immune function.

Upon completion of the degree in Exercise Physiology, the student will:

1. Be prepared to communicate the role of nutrition in health, exercise, and athletics.
2. Demonstrate advanced knowledge and competencies fundamental to assessing, understanding, and communicating cardiovascular concepts and laboratory skills.
3. Demonstrate an understanding and ability to compare and contrast health, fitness and exercise related research methods, designs, statistics and implications for healthy lifestyle.
4. Demonstrate requisite professional knowledge and competencies required of different exercise physiology career opportunities in the public sector.
5. Become an ASEP board certified member.
6. Demonstrate requisite anatomical knowledge and cardiovascular physiology competencies fundamental to the exercise physiology profession.
7. Demonstrate requisite knowledge and application of mind-body interventions in promoting healthy lifestyles.
8. Demonstrate requisite communication skills fundamental to leadership positions in the profession of exercise physiology.

9. Demonstrate critical thinking skills fundamental to articulating personal and professional values.

10. Acknowledge and apply the ASEP Code of Ethics in all aspects of the profession and work.

The Best Exercise Physiologist

Who is the best exercise physiologist you know? Of course, if you are not in college right now, this is a very hard question to answer. If you are in college, which of your professors would you want to be like? Maybe you still do not know enough about them to make a decision. Either way, here is something to think about.

You probably will not identify the personal trainer at the local gym. For one thing, that person may not have graduated from high school. Also, how can you trust one of the 300 or so weekend and online fitness certifications? Most people would not. Healthcare is just that, the care of someone's health. It is too important to turn over to unqualified individuals. Yet, this is being done everyday because the public is not fully informed.

ASEP board certified exercise physiologists are competent and caring professionals. They understand the word "credibility." Also, they have internalized the understanding that healthcare professionals are part of the healthcare system. They must be honest, trustworthy, and ethical in their dealings with clients. After all, they are caregivers, much like a nurse or a physical therapist. Now, you know the rest of the story!

Part Four

Healthcare Professionals

Being a healthcare professional is never an accident; it is always the result of planned academic effort.

In the quiet hours when we are alone and there is nobody to tell us what fine fellows we are, we come sometimes upon a moment in which we wonder, not how much money we are earning, nor how famous we have become, but what good we are doing. – A. A. Milne

Chapter Thirteen

Exercise Physiologists as Professionals

Exercise physiologists have just begun to think of themselves as professionals.

The healthcare revolution is shaping the future of health and fitness delivery systems. Fortunately, exercise physiologists are qualified to be an integral part of the new delivery of healthcare. That is, by being academically prepared and proactive on behalf of lifestyle issues, they are in an excellent position to help with health and fitness problems. This means there will be new career opportunities. Those who cannot change or adapt will not be recognized as credible healthcare professionals. This is why it is so important for students to evolve with new skills, new values and sound knowledge, and new methods of applying what they know to benefit society.

In professional terms, the crisis before the so-called exercise professionals (i.e., the fitness instructors and personal trainers) is the lack of a credible academic degree, board certification and standards of practice. This is why the *American Society of Exercise Physiologists* is so important. It is the professional organization of exercise physiologists with the mission to enable all exercise physiologists to be successful healthcare practitioners. As a student and as a future professional, the organization strengthens your capacity to shift from yesterday's thinking as an "exercise professional" to today's professional title of "Exercise Physiologists."

Led first by the ASEP Board of Directors and, then, by the Board of Directors of *The Center for Exercise Physiology-online*, exercise physiologists have their own professional "board certification" (i.e., the "Exercise Physiologist Certified" – the EPC exam). The certification not only defines the exercise physiologist of the 21st century, it also sets the stage for providing professional healthcare services. In other words, the EPC is designed to protect the welfare of the client.

Board of Certification

The members of the Board of Certification have three important functions. First, they are responsible for conducting the "Exercise Physiologist Certified" (EPC) examination for exercise physiologists. Second, they are responsible for the re-certification requirements for certified exercise physiologists. Third, they protect the interest of the public by defining the acceptable standards of professional practice. The Board of Certification [1] has declared that the "professional" exercise physiologist requires certification according to the EPC certification procedures, and that exercise physiologists who are academically qualified and certified as EPCs to practice exercise physiology are qualified to provide community-based high-tech and comprehensive hands-on healthcare services. It is the established way among other healthcare professions of saying that exercise physiologists are credible professionals.

What Does "Examination" Mean?

Exercise physiology *examination* includes taking a relevant history, practical laboratory evaluation, and assessment of the musculoskeletal system and cardiovascular system using standard laboratory equipment, exercise tests, exercise programs, and risk factor modification and/or measurements to assist in evaluating the client's overt and/or objective responses, signs, and/or symptoms. Such tests include, but are not limited to:

1. Tests that measure percent body fat, lean muscle tissue ratio, range of motion (flexibility), muscle strength, endurance, work, and power.
2. Tests that assist in overall analysis of the central (i.e., $Q = HR \times SV$) and/or peripheral (a-vO_2 diff) components of oxygen consumption and energy expenditure.

3. Tests for pulmonary function (such as expired ventilation, tidal volume, and frequency of breaths).

4. Tests that determine cardiovascular function, that set the stage for exercise prescription for individuals with metabolic disorders, including but not limited to [2]:

   - deficiencies of the cardiovascular system
   - diabetes
   - lipid disorders
   - hypertension
   - cancer
   - cystic fibrosis
   - chronic obstructive and restrictive pulmonary disease
   - arthritis
   - organ transplant
   - peripheral vascular disease
   - obesity.

5. Tests that include treadmill test protocols in conjunction with exercise electrocardiography (ECG) to identify the heart rate and ECG responses at rest, during submaximal, and maximal graded exercise programs in addition to specific contraindications to continuing to exercise.

Note: The examination of heart patients, as an example of one type of disability, during stress testing does not include examining any person for the purpose of diagnosing any disease or organic condition. Nothing herein, however, is intended to preclude exercise physiologists from stress testing and/or using a variety of different bicycle and treadmill ergometers in assessing and/or educating subjects otherwise with or without known disease and/or cardiovascular disability.

What Does "Instruction" Mean?

Exercise physiology *instruction* includes providing educational, consultative, or other advisory services for the purpose of helping the public with issues and concerns regarding fundamental and scientific information about mind-body health and fitness, particularly with regards to matters that are believed to develop and maintain health, fitness, rehabilitation, and/or athletics. Instruction includes, but is not limited to, the following topics:

1. The acute physiological responses to exercise.
2. Chronic physiological adaptations to training
3. Designing resistance training programs
4. Measuring energy expenditure at rest and during exercise
5. Hormonal regulation and/or metabolic adaptations to training
6. Cardiorespiratory regulation and adaptation during exercise
7. Exercising at altitude, underwater, and in space
8. Optimizing sports training through the use of responsible nutrition
9. Body composition and optimal body weight analysis and physical activity
10. Growth and development of athletes, including aging and gender issues
11. Biochemistry of exercise and training
12. Preventing cardiovascular disease through exercise
13. Thermal regulation during exercise
14. Prescription of exercise for health and exercise
15. Biomechanical aspects of posture and sports
16. Physiological assessment of human movement
17. Stress testing protocols for athletics and special populations
18. Resting and exercise electrocardiography
19. Mind-body techniques for reducing stress and increasing running economy
20. Physiological assessments during different body positions

What Does "Analysis and Treatment" Mean?

Exercise physiology *analysis and treatment* include hands-on contact to perform specific laboratory tests, with specific expectations for 'treatment' measures and activities, including but not limited to, the following areas:

1. Range of motion exercises
2. Muscle strength and muscle endurance exercises
3. Lean muscle tissue-fat analysis
4. Musculoskeletal and/or postural exercises
5. Sports nutrition programs in athletics
6. Sports biomechanics in work places
7. Stress management exercises
8. Sports training and development programs
9. Cardiac and pulmonary rehabilitation (including, but not limited to:
   - Development of the such programs
   - Supervision of testing
   - Development of exercise prescription
   - Education and counseling of patients
10. Exercise physiology instruction that pertains to all forms of sports training and athletics

The New Exercise Physiology Model

It is clear that the healthcare concerns in the United States present challenges to exercise physiologists and all healthcare professionals. They will find themselves exploring new healthcare business opportunities along with many unfamiliar policies and procedures. For clients of all ages, this means getting used to new ways of thinking about exercise physiology beyond the notion of "acute and chronic changes to regular exercise."

As a student in exercise physiology, you will find yourself thinking more like nurses and physical therapists than like personal trainers in gyms. You will find yourself exploring the historical edges of what was the discipline of exercise

167

physiology, and the new unfolding profession of exercise physiology based on entrepreneurial thinking and application of healthcare concepts. You will also find yourself adapting to the changes and challenges of the future. All students will realize the importance of developing leadership skills and break-through thinking, including the ability to [3]:

- Embrace 100% the new exercise physiology credentials (e.g., the EPC exam), whereby other professionals will automatically recognize your path towards professionalism, accountability, and credibility.

- Adapt with new thinking and emotional flexibility to circumstances in the public sector still undergoing shifts in old thinking to the new priorities of the 21st century healthcare issues and concerns.

- Think outside of the box so that there is opportunity to view exercise physiology as a business within its own professional and ethical constraints.

- Stay the course in the pursuit of your own professionalism and your contribution to the professional development of exercise physiology.

- Continue the transformation of exercise physiology from just an athletic view to a healthcare profession through inspiring others to embrace the ASEP philosophy.

Chapter Fourteen

Exercise Physiologists as Healthcare Professionals?

Exercise physiology is a public service of significant altruistic activities.

Today, the number of healthcare professionals is higher than most caregivers would expect. Aside from physicians, nurses, dentists and supportive services, there are dozens of different health occupations. This figure is growing, especially with the holistic healers who rely on a variety of alternative medical services. The increased specialization in healthcare is partly responsible for the growth in caregivers.

While many independent practitioners may choose to specialize in healthcare, exercise physiologists are likely to be employed in almost every healthcare setting. Some will work primarily in the clinical realm such as cardiac rehabilitation. Others will work to improve fitness and athletics. Still others will be employed in the business sector. They will be healthcare professionals with a desire to evaluate and counsel individuals in their "store front" businesses in much the same way a psychologist, dentist, chiropractor, and others have practiced for decades.

Regardless of where exercise physiologists find employment, they will need to work collaboratively with many professionals. Exercise physiologists will need to be familiar with the following healthcare professionals who are committed to health, fitness, rehabilitation, athletics, and wellness.

Athletic Trainers

Athletic trainers graduate from an academic program accredited by the *Commission on Accreditation of Allied Health Education Programs* [1].

Graduates from accredited institutions sit for the *National Athletic Trainers' Association* certification examination [2]. The exam is used in most states that require licensure. After completing the exam, athletic trainers work primarily with athletic teams at the high school, college, and professional level. Many athletic trainers also work in sports medicine clinics alongside other healthcare professionals (e.g., exercise physiologists, physical therapist, and nurses) in the care and prevention of illness and injury related to sports participation and exercise.

Biomechanists

The biomechanist combines classical mechanical and biological perspectives with emphasis on human movement, sports related injuries, muscular skeletal system, and athletic performance. They are responsible for understanding and applying both academic and industrial ergonomic applications. There are several national and international organizations that support biomechanics as an integral part of exercise physiology, sports medicine, and orthopedics.

Biomechanists draw upon the study of the structure and function of biology, physics, engineering, and computer science. Advancements in the field are closely tied to new computer software, specialized cameras, force transducers, force platforms, and other laboratory equipment that allow for a comprehensive, 3-dimensional analysis of human movement. By understanding the internal and external forces involved in human motion, athletes and coaches can maximize safety, effectiveness, and efficiency during human movement. Links to websites for specific information about biomechanics include:

1. *American Society of Biomechanics* [http://www.asb-biomech.org/]
2. *Biomechanics World-Wide* [http://www.per.ualberta.ca/biomechanics/]
3. *International Society of Biomechanics* [http://www.isb.ri.ccf.org/], and
4. *International Society of Biomechanics in Sports* [http://www.uni-stuttgart.de/External/isbs/]

Chiropractors

Doctors of Chiropractic (DC) are physicians concerned with human health and disease processes. They have special training in spinal mechanics, neurological, and muscular relationships. The "spinal adjustment" is their primary treatment method along with dietary advice and physiotherapeutic counsel.

Chiropractors use standard physical examination procedures (e.g., consultation, case history, laboratory analyses, and x-rays) to diagnose improper functioning of the musculoskeletal areas of the body. Doctors of Chiropractic also place emphasis on exercise and nutritional programs that have a positive influence on lifestyle and wellness promotion, including mental health. Several important links to websites for more information include:

1. *American Chiropractic Association* [http://www.amerchiro.org/]

2. *Chiroweb.com* [http://www.chiroweb.com/], and

3. *International Chiropractors Association* [http://www.chiropractic.org/]

Dietitians

Professionals with an interest in food science and human nutrition include dietitians, home economists and food technologists. Dietitians are responsible for the selection of foods for specific diets. They also counsel patients in and out of the hospital setting, clinics, public health facilities, school systems, and the patient's own home to prevent disease and improve health and fitness. Dietitians interested in sports

evaluate   dietary | http://www.eatright.org/cps/rde/xchg/ada/hs.xsl/index.html

intake of athletes

to maximize physical performance.

The *American Dietetic Association* is the nation's largest organization of food and nutrition professionals. The organization serves the public by promoting optimal nutrition, health and well-being. The *American Dietetic Association* and its *Commission on Dietetic Registration* have adopted a voluntary, enforceable Code of Ethics. This code, entitled the Code of Ethics for the Profession of

Dietetics, challenges all members, registered dietitians, and dietetic technicians, registered, to uphold ethical principles. The enforcement process for the Code of Ethics establishes a fair system to deal with complaints about members and credentialed practitioners from peers or the public.

Medical Doctors

Doctors of Medicine (MD) practice diagnosis and treatment of disease and injury. After graduation from medical school, most MDs choose a graduate medical education (preparation) for specialties as their field of practice. They prescribe drugs, use routine diagnostic measures, and perform surgery.

A sports medicine physician is trained in the art and science of injuries sustained in athletics, including prevention, diagnosis, and treatment. Most medical doctors work in hospitals or clinics. The link to the *American Medical Association* is: http://www.ama-assn.org/

Nurses

The *American Nurses Association* (http://www.nursingworld.org/) is the primary organization for nurses in the United States. It serves some 200,000 members. Registered nurses provide care to the sick and injured. They promote health and wellness, and assist in providing holistic care, including but not limited to, emotional, mental, and social needs of individuals. Although nurses are primarily employed in hospitals, they also work in nursing homes, healthcare agencies, doctor's offices, healthcare settings, and industrial complexes.

Health Educators

Health educators are concerned with the prevention of disease and injury. They help people change their way of living toward a more optimal balance of physical, emotional, social, and intellectual health and fitness. To promote and facilitate changes in the lifestyle behavior of patients and clients (such as sedentary lifestyle, alcohol, drug abuse, and tobacco use, and stress), health educators work in educational settings, community agencies, medical and clinical institutions, corporate and private worksites, government agencies, private industry, and insurance companies. Website links to information related to this field include:

1. *American Public Health Association* [http://www.apha.org/]
2. *Association for Worksite Health Promotion* [http://www.awhp.org/], and
3. *National Wellness Institute* [http://www.nationalwellness.org/]

Occupational Therapists

The occupational therapist plans and directs purposeful activity in the promotion and maintenance of health, the prevention of workplace injuries and disabilities, and the evaluation of physical and/or psychosocial behaviors. They use a variety of self-care, work activities, play and social activities, educational, and vocational principles to improve the occupational abilities and independent functions of workers.

For clients with a physical disability (such as, strokes, mental illness, developmental disabilities, cerebral palsy, and burns), the primary focus of occupational therapy is with such activities as dressing, grooming, bathing, and eating. Then, the plan of care is centered more on caring for the client's home and family concerns, identifying, and helping with employment. Job opportunities are found in rehabilitation hospitals and centers, nursing homes, physician private practice and clinics, home health agencies, mental health centers, public schools, community centers, teaching, and research.

The primary link to information related to occupational therapy is the *American Occupational Therapy Association* [http:///www.aota.org/].

Physical Therapists

The restoration of function and the prevention of disability following disease, musculoskeletal injury, or loss of a body part are the professional concerns and practice of physical therapists. The physical therapist's program of treatment is based on the medical doctor's prescription. The goal is to encourage motion, strengthen the musculoskeletal system, and improve the patient's performance of activities required in daily living. In giving therapy, they use exercise, cold, heat, crutches, prosthetics, walks, ultrasound, and massage.

Physical therapists practice in private physical therapy offices, industrial health centers, sport and athletic centers, nursing homes, home health agencies, schools and community health centers, research institutions, and in educational settings. The primary link to information about physical therapy is the *American Physical Therapy Association* [http://www.apta.org/].

Sports Medicine

The practice of sports medicine is multidisciplinary, including primarily athletic trainers and sports physicians. Other professionals involved in sports medicine include physical therapists, exercise physiologists, physician assistants, and other allied health professionals. Sports medicine professionals are also interested in improving and maintaining the capacity of the cardiorespiratory system as well as the integrity of the musculoskeletal system for exercise and sports training.

There are two organizations of sports medicine professionals. The *American College of Sports Medicine* is a multidisciplinary organization of professionals from a variety of educational backgrounds and training. The *National Athletic Trainers' Association* is *the* professional organization of athletic trainers. The Internet link to ACSM is [http://www.acsm.org/], and to the NATA organization is [http://www.nata.org/].

There are many healthcare workers not described in this chapter. It would be unrealistic to attempt a description of the more than 200 occupations and professions across the healthcare field, such as:

- Respiratory Therapists
- Nuclear Medicine Technologists
- Physician Assistants
- Rehabilitation Counselors

- Alternative Therapists
- Electrocardiograph Technicians (to name just a few).

This list is obviously not complete and, in fact, it is expanding. It is also clear that members of these specialties, including exercise physiologists are part of the healthcare services in hospitals and clinics.

Chapter Fifteen

Exercise Physiologists as College Teachers

It has become apparent that all exercise physiologists are not professors, but without them we would get no where.

To become an academic exercise physiologist requires a commitment to critical thinking and hands-on laboratory experiences and an understanding of scientific thinking and application to real life events. Of course, the academic exercise physiologist must also have the determination to obtain the doctorate degree or, as is more commonly called, the PhD degree (Doctor of Philosophy). There are other doctorate degrees that work just as well (e.g., the Doctor of Education, EdD and the Doctor of Arts, DA).

The academic position is traditionally recognized as a doctorate position with emphasis on research and publishing. You may be surprised that research is so important, but it is actually a very important part that determines how exercise physiologists and other professionals perform their work. That is why exercise physiologists who teach at the college or university level are expected to do research. Of course, they are expected to present their work at national meetings too. Then, they are expected to publish scientific papers and books.

Professors with other doctorate degrees also do research and publish their work. Aside from several relatively minor historical differences, there are no serious issues between the EdD and the PhD professionals. This is also true with other doctorate degrees, including the Doctor of Physical Education (DPE) degree. Perhaps, during the next decade, exercise physiologists will push for the Doctor of Exercise Physiology (DEP) degree. After all,

> **The Doctor of Exercise Physiology is the preferred degree.**

philosophically speaking, it is the right thing to do. It would be comparable to the

Doctor of Physical Therapy (DPT) degree for entry level into the healthcare profession. The DEPs will still engage in research activities just like all other doctorate prepared professionals who work at the college or university level.

The following is a checklist used to determine if a person is suited for the profession. You may find it interesting. Why not complete it.

Yes   No

1. I look forward to working with people.

2. Research is important to me.

3. I like taking physiological data and translating it to real applications.

4. I am confident that exercise physiology is a scientific field of work.

5. I am known as a person who can be trusted; a person with integrity.

6. It is important to have the opportunity to publish my work in journals.

7. I enjoy working with clients and helping them solve fitness problems

8. I am able to prioritize personal and professional responsibilities.

9. I have good communication and hands-on skills.

10. I like anatomy and physiology courses.

11. I know that work in exercise physiology involves laboratory testing.

12. I like to read articles published in scientific journals.

13. I enjoy using metabolic equipment to assess fitness and endurance.

14. I look forward to four years of college to be an exercise physiologist.

To score this assessment instrument, give two points for a yes response to items 1, 3, 4, 7, 9, 11, and 13. These items have been chosen as the seven key statements for a potential student to become a successful exercise physiologist. Give one point to a yes response for each of the other seven items. If your total score is 15 or essentially 70% of a possible score of 21, regardless of the combination of "2" and "1" you are a good candidate for college work.

Exercise physiology is an evolving healthcare profession that serves many different and diverse health, fitness, and rehabilitative needs of people all ages. The practice of exercise physiology includes working with people to assess their physiological needs by way of metabolic and cardiovascular analyzers that are unique to exercise physiology laboratories. Exercise physiologists use scientific problem-solving techniques to facilitate interpersonal communication. They are interested in the correct analysis, care, education, and support of the client during fitness training or rehabilitation.

A career as a college teacher consists of teaching academic courses and doing research on college-aged students and/or athletes. It is also very likely that the academic exercise physiologist may test and rehabilitate adults with coronary artery disease. Very likely, they will supervise patients in cardiac or pulmonary rehabilitation programs housed in hospitals or on a college or university campus. And, increasingly, more exercise physiologists are directing exercise programs for children with special health needs or special populations of individuals with a variety of musculoskeletal concerns.

Perhaps, it should be pointed out that most academic prepared exercise physiologists have a doctorate degree in kinesiology or a related field with an *"emphasis"* in exercise science or exercise physiology. It may be several decades before the majority of the doctorate programs will graduate exercise physiologists will an academic major in exercise physiology at the doctorate level.

Graduates of these programs are usually interested in providing students with a scientific and comprehensive background in a variety of physiologically related courses they teach, such as:

- Physiology of Exercise
- Biomechanics
- Advanced Exercise Physiology
- Cardiovascular Physiology

179

- Biochemistry of Exercise
- Cardiopulmonary Rehabilitation
- Gross Anatomy (with cadaver dissection)
- Physiological Assessment
- Exercise Testing
- Electrocardiography
- Sports Nutrition
- Research and Statistics
- Seminars in Exercise Physiology
- Physiology of Aging

Improvement in the student's academic course work has been a major topic for several years now. Many facets of the student's education involve the capture of the right combination of courses and research topics. As stated earlier, it is realistic to expect that not too far in the near future students will enroll in the Doctor of Exercise Physiology (DEP) degree [1]. It is noteworthy that the basic tenets of the DEP degree, namely content, laboratory, and research experiences have been identified and published elsewhere. As times permits, you may want to refer to the *Professionalization of Exercise Physiologyonline* electronic journal for selected articles on this topic. It is essential that more work is done in this area for all the obvious reasons. It is also essential that the degree is eventually implemented within the exercise physiology profession.

Chapter Sixteen

Ethical Issues in Exercise Physiology

It is not easy being ethical and even a code of ethics does not guarantee ethical behavior, but it is a start.

Welcome to the ethical side of exercise physiology. Every career has an ethical side to it. Exercise physiology is no different from other professions. Healthcare practitioners must be aware of what is ethical behavior in their own profession. As an exercise physiologist, making the right personal and professional decision is not always easy. This chapter presents the ASEP Exercise Physiologist's Code of Ethics [1].

While some students may find the study of ethics either unnecessary or confusing, it is the backbone of ethical thinking. It is important that students learn to think straight and accept responsibility for their actions. To think straight means that you can safely and productively contribute to the health of those you care for.

Ethical thinking and professional behavior are guides to thinking straight. Both are the critical to any healthcare profession. Therefore, it is important that you read carefully the

Ethical issues cannot be overlooked.

following tips that will assist you in thinking right. Use these tips along with the ASEP Code of Ethics to guide your personal and professional thinking and behavior.

Find a Straight-Thinking Mentor

But, the question is this: "Is he a straight thinker?"

Exercise physiologists have not always had a "professional practice." It is probably true that most exercise physiologists do not no why they need a document that itemizes what they do. Nonetheless, it is imperative that the ASEP "practice" is discussed in class, at conferences, and at meetings [2]. An ASEP faculty member or mentor can be a positive force in helping students understand the new direction exercise physiology has taken as a healthcare profession with a scientific and applied interest in athletics.

Create a Support Group

> Knowing is not enough; we must be willing to listen to others.

Speak with other students in your program who are interested in professional credentials. The strengths that associate with accountability, and the benefits of coming together to talk and write about the professional development of exercise physiology are important and go a long way, respectively. Remember, it is important to be prepared. You may want to create a support group of friends, students, or colleagues. The most successful students are generally those who are psychologically and otherwise prepared for the transition from college to the real world. Remember: Getting a job requires work!

Be Prepared to Ignore Pessimistic Thinkers

> There is nothing wrong with different points of view. The strange thing is that we so often forget to be prepared.

All professions have members who disagree about the path of professionalism. Where possible, ignore pessimistic thinkers. Associate with those who believe exercise physiologists ought to belong to their own professional organization [3]. Most importantly, learn to support those who are working on your behalf (i.e., the ASEP organization). You may want to think about what they have done on your behalf is not new, but it is necessary. Credibility and professional accountability must be taken seriously [4]. Remember: Every established healthcare profession has been doing it for decades!

Believe in Yourself

> The reward of a thing well done is to have done it. – R. Waldo Emerson

Students are eager to learn, and college teachers are full of ideas. Some of the ideas and the work involved may be a reality shock for students. Seek the aid of those who understand the importance of believing in yourself. They are also the students who are more likely to clarify the reasons for the ideas and the long hours of study.

In short, the idea of depending on someone else for your best thinking makes little sense. Life is full of challenges. Learn to stay the course and believe in yourself [5]. You will find it a little hard at first, but learn it. Learn to listen to yourself. After all, you can make a difference by just listening and practice positive thinking.

Find Your Niche

> The secret of joy in work is finding your niche.

There are many opportunities for a student to lay the foundation for professional growth. To begin with, take responsibility for your niche as a student. It may be research or a specific kind of research or mentoring other students about the work that exercise physiologists do. The best way to succeed is to take one step at a time, then, find your niche and go after your dream [6].

You may say, "Oh my gosh, how am I going to do that?" Well, the answer comes with effort, action, and conviction. Even the successful students did not start without a vision or an idea. As a general rule of thumb, your first priority is to identify the academic major. Everything generally falls into place after that. So, do not waste your time in fear of making a decision. Do it anyway. Nothing has to be forever. Should you decide to change your major, do it. It is not uncommon for students to feel that way during the first few years of school.

The Exercise Physiology Code of Ethics

> The rewards of being part of a profession do not come easily; it requires
> discipline and straight thinking.

The significance of the Code of Ethics is that both students and professionals in the study and application of exercise physiology to health, fitness, exercise, preventive and rehabilitative services (and athletics) can turn to it for guidance in their professional conduct. Adherence to the Code is expected. It is based on the belief that exercise physiologists are self-regulated, critical thinkers who are accountable and responsible for their high quality competence in the practice and the delivery of exercise physiology concepts, ideas, and services.

The following 10 Codes with a brief "clarification point" represent the first-ever steps to hold exercise physiologists accountable to ethical thinking and practice:

1. Exercise physiologists should accurately communicate and provide health and fitness, educational, preventive, rehabilitative, and/or research services equitably to all individuals regardless of social or economic status, age, gender, race, ethnicity, national origin, religion, disability, diverse values, attitudes, or opinions.

   - Either purposefully or inadvertently, if an exercise physiologist fails to communicate accurately and equitably with a client in whatever capacity or condition, it will very likely be viewed as unethical.

2. Exercise physiologists should be responsible and accountable for individual non-medical judgments and decisions about health and fitness, preventive, rehabilitative, educational, and/or research services.

   - If exercise physiologists fail to be responsible and accountable for the information shared with clients, they are likely to be viewed as unethical.

184

3. Exercise physiologists should maintain high quality professional competence through continued study of the latest laboratory techniques and research in preventive and rehabilitative services.

- Exercise physiologists are responsible to their clients for high quality professional competence. Failure to maintain competence by communicating misinformation may make exercise physiologists liable for unethical behavior and practice of exercise physiology.

4. Exercise physiologists are expected to conduct health and fitness, preventive, rehabilitative, educational, research, and other scholarly activities in accordance with recognized legal, scientific, ethical, and professional standards.

- Failure to adhere to recognized legal, scientific, ethical, and professional standards is unethical. Examples might include the publishing of articles, research or otherwise, that promote findings that are inconsistent with recognized standards of ethical conduct.

5. Exercise physiologists should respect and protect the privacy, rights, and dignity of all individuals by not disclosing health and fitness, rehabilitative, and/or research information unless required by law or when confidentiality jeopardizes the health and safety of others.

- Unless required by law, exercise physiologists violate the trusts of their clients if they share contents of personal tests and results with others.

6. Exercise physiologists are expected to call attention to unprofessional health and fitness, preventive, rehabilitative, educational, and/or research services that result from incompetent, unethical, or illegal professional behavior.

- It is the responsibility of the exercise physiologist to call attention to the unprofessional behavior of colleagues who promote unethical practices. This may be in the form of athletes or clients who are looking for a quick fix to their health and fitness problems. The behavior may also be found in the context of what is said in a presentation at meetings or within the content of published articles.

7. Exercise physiologists should contribute to the ongoing development and integrity of the profession by being responsive to, mutually supportive, and accurately communicating academic and other qualifications to colleagues and associates in the health and fitness, preventive, rehabilitative, educational and/or research services and programs.

   - When exercise physiologists refuse or fail to contribute to the professional development and integrity of the profession or support the ASEP Code of Ethics, their behavior may be viewed as unethical.

8. Exercise physiologists should participate in the profession's efforts to establish high quality services by avoiding conflicts of interest and endorsement of products in the health and fitness, preventive, and/or rehabilitative services and programs.

   - Endorsements of products (such as equipment, drugs, and sports supplements), including consulting activities that run counter to the best interest of the public and/or athletes may be viewed as unethical behavior, depending on the circumstances and the potential for conflicts of interest.

9. Exercise physiologists should participate in and encourage critical discourse to reflect the collective knowledge and practice within the exercise physiology profession to protect the public from misinformation, incompetence, and unethical acts.

   - Exercise physiologists who communicate misinformation to their clients are guilty of unethical behavior.

10. Exercise physiologists should provide health and fitness, preventive, rehabilitative, and/or educational interventions grounded in a theoretical

framework supported by research that enables a healthy lifestyle through choice.

- The exercise physiologist's body of knowledge is founded on solid scientific research information, data, and findings. The failure to promote solid scientific thinking is unethical.

For more information about ethics, ethical thinking, and professional values, refer to the following articles published in either the PEPonline journal or the JPEP journal. The URL for each article is included with the title:

http://faculty.css.edu/tboone2/asep/Professionalization.html

- **The Future of Exercise Physiology: A Matter of Ethics**
  http://faculty.css.edu/tboone2/asep/MatterOfEthics.html
- **Cheating in Sports: What Should Exercise Physiologists Think?**
  http://faculty.css.edu/tboone2/asep/CheatingWhatExercisePhysiologistsThink.html
- **The Professional Practice of Exercise Physiology and Ethical Thinking**
  http://faculty.css.edu/tboone2/asep/ProfessionalPracticeANDethicalTHINKING.html
- **Ethical Thinking: What Is It and Why Does It Matter?**
  http://faculty.css.edu/tboone2/asep/EthicalThinkingANDexercisephysiology.html
- **Exercise Physiology Quackery and Consumer Fraud**
  http://faculty.css.edu/tboone2/asep/ExercisePhysiologyQuackery.html
- **Introduction to Professional Ethics**
  http://faculty.css.edu/tboone2/asep/ProfessionalETHICS.html
- **Organizational Code of Moral Principles and Values**
  http://faculty.css.edu/tboone2/asep/OrganizationalCodeOfMoralPrinciples.html
- **The Sports Supplements Disagreement: A Call for a Dialogue About Values and Obligations of University Teachers**
  http://faculty.css.edu/tboone2/asep/TheSportsSupplementsDisagreement.doc

- **Dietary "Sports" Supplements: The University Teacher's Role in Teaching Values?**
  http://faculty.css.edu/tboone2/asep/TeachingVALUES.html
- **Medical Ethics in Exercise Physiology**
  http://www.exercisephysiologists.com/MedicalEthics/index.html

Part Five

The Exercise Physiology Niche

The secret to a profession is knowing what its members are really trying to accomplish.

The first responsibility of a leader is to define reality. – Max DePree

Chapter Seventeen

Understanding Healthcare

Anyone who understands healthcare knows that it is a business.

Although there are many different kinds of healthcare professionals, the strategies for addressing the problems of cost and access are very similar. In spite of the impressive accomplishments in healthcare, the perplexing problem is that the policy makers and care managers are often driven by economic and political factors. This is not the case with exercise physiology! It is not influenced or driven by economic or political agendas.

The private sector is replete with professionals (and organizations) with unique treatments and proposals for healthcare problems. Many professionals seek public support for funds and recognition of their programs, while others do not. Their understanding of healthcare and management of lifestyle risk factors for diseases and dysfunctions may come from less scientifically documented resources. The mystery embedded in some programs suggests that a certain inherent danger exists in using such care. This is not the case with exercise physiology! It is defined by a specialized body of knowledge derived from scientific research and critical thinking.

Rather than encouraging clients and patients to maintain blind faith in the exercise physiologist's capability, the state of the exercise physiology body of knowledge justifies it as a serious scientific study. This is important because the long-held assumptions by

> **Scientists who view exercise physiology as a healthcare profession understand that it is based on scientific thinking and standards.**

scientists are driven by the huge expenditure of energy engaged in responsible thinking and publishing. This is exactly the case with exercise physiology!

> **The future influence and involvement of exercise physiologists at all levels of their education on health (mental and physical) and medical care are great.**

Exercise physiology professionals are at the core of using "exercise" in the prevention and treatment of diseases and the promotion of good healthcare. Much of the information that is provided the public via a large array of healthcare facts and services is shaped by the nature of exercise physiology research. This is not the case with some unconventional health therapies, although it should be. Fortunately, "exercise physiology as medicine" is not identified with the various forms of other so-called medicine. Exercise physiologists believe this is as it should be. Few exercise physiologists offer their services solely for monetary gain.

From mental health to better quality and costs of exercise healthcare, to new services and fee-for-service reimbursement arrangements, to significant lifestyle advances in infants to aging adults, the multi-faceted care opportunities by the exercise physiologist are a consequence of a comprehensive array of integrated educational and hands-on experiences and application to real-world problems [1]. This is exactly as it should be, and it is what the accredited exercise physiology programs promote, communicate, and recommend. Hence, the benefits to society of investing in an academic education in exercise physiology are unquestionably rewarding and effective.

For these reasons and more, the growth of exercise physiology is expected to increase. Much of the estimated work will deal directly with the aging of the United States population. Imagine, by the year 2050, it is estimated that 30% of the population will be over 65 years of age. The size of this age group is especially problematic as is the shortage of board certified exercise physiologists. The issue, of course, before the private sector is whether the exercise physiologist that is hired for personal health enhancement is board certified. This is exactly the concern of the *American Society of Exercise Physiologists*.

192

Here, it is important to recognize the seriousness of the ASEP organization and its leadership role in the professional development of exercise physiology as a healthcare profession. The overall burden on society is much less when fitness and exercise matters are under the direction of professionals with high technology and physiological care and expertise. This is, in fact, the basic reason and issues underlying the founding of the ASEP organization. More students and faculty should be inspired to join the organization. Improving communication among all exercise physiologists is critical in creating a coherent and credible profession.

> **It is clear that clients are uncomfortable with employees who do not have a professional education.**

Otherwise, the pressure placed on the board certified exercise physiologists, who work in the same physical environments with non-exercise physiologists, will be enormous. But, in fairness to exercise physiology, it is important to point out that the strained relationship between professionals and non-professionals is not specific to exercise physiology. It crosses an increasingly diverse array of healthcare disciplines and medical occupations.

As an allied health practitioner, the exercise physiologist plays a major role in the monitoring of cardiovascular function (via exercise tests), the assessment of treatment interventions (e.g., exercise), the rehabilitation of medical conditions (particularly in regards to heart patients), and the prevention of disease and/or health maintenance through patient education and counseling activities.

Also, with increasing specialization of the exercise physiologist, there will be increased career opportunities in all areas of healthcare (e.g., obesity, osteoporosis, mental depression, muscular weakness, diabetes, and so forth). The explosion in

> **Predicting the future is not easy, but it is certain that exercise physiologists will be a vital contributor to healthcare in the United States.**

exercise physiology technology and advances in physiological assessments will fuel significant breakthroughs in the understanding of how to live a more productive, disease-free lifestyle. As a result, there will be a growing acceptance of exercise physiologists across many diverse fields of work.

Chapter Eighteen

The Exercise Physiology Healthcare Clinic

The greatest thing in this world is not so much where we are, but in what direction we are moving. -- Oliver Wendell Holmes

Health is important to everyone. Everyone is concerned with the health of their family members. Life itself requires a high level of maintenance. The capacity to perform physically is linked to the client's physical and mental status. It is known that there is a predisposition to different diseases that are linked to the stress factors at home and at work. Life is a struggle to stay healthy.

Toward that end, health promotion is part of a huge body of professionals who belong to established provider systems. Historically, the providers are located in hospitals, clinics, and a variety of treatment centers with diverse interventions. The use of the providers often results from not being healthy. And, everyone knows that failed health often comes at a high financial cost.

Excrcise physiologists can help reduce this healthcare costs by promoting positive healthy lifestyles. Obviously, the objective of good health must be grounded in regular exercise and mental

Exercise physiologists are "exercise therapists."

strategies for dealing with stress and anxiety. After all, the relationship between exercise and health has been recognized for many decades. Exercise physiologists are educated to initiate multilevel interventions to bring about healthcare changes.

However, only by examining aggregates of lifestyle and behavior issues can individuals understand the combination of factors that associate with dysfunction and disease. In other words, health is more than just exercise. This is exactly the "breaking news" exercise physiologists want to share with the public sector. They know that good health is linked to a positive and stable lifestyle. Exercise physiology researchers and educators have pointed this out for decades.

The ASEP organization is central to the commitment of exercise physiologists as healthcare professionals in the community [1]. This shift from more traditional roles of work as technicians to the community with increased professional responsibility and involvement in helping individuals singly and collectively improve healthcare is important to the professional development of exercise physiology. From this effort will come an increase in career options. The willingness to make this shift from the gym to the larger community is a daunting task.

The Challenge to College Teachers

> To become what we are, we must release the image of exercise physiology that is within us.

The challenge before academic exercise physiologists is to develop an integrated, scientifically-based healthcare curriculum solidly grounded in exercise physiology knowledge and professional practice. To achieve this objective, the faculty will increasingly get more involved in curriculum reform [2]. As a result, they will spend less time teaching non-exercise physiology courses such as motor learning, "how to teach" different activities, and other traditional physical education courses This will provide them more time to spend on exercise physiology courses.

Also, students will need courses in management and systems thinking, business policy and procedures, and computer skills. They will need to understand private practice. This will require the faculty to make significant changes in how exercise physiology is taught. Adherence to the ASEP definitions of what is exercise physiology and who is an exercise physiologist will place a primary focus on improving health through critical reflection and cognitive strategies.

196

Required Shift in Thinking

The shift in thinking occurs on the coat tails of decades of exercise physiology research [3]. As stated earlier, the healthcare link is solidly fixed to a specialized body of knowledge that is uniquely exercise physiology. Like other healthcare professionals, there is increasingly less ambiguity with the question: "What is the exercise physiology scope of practice?" But, this does not mean that the theory and practice that underpins exercise physiology as a healthcare profession are completely defined or even accepted by all members of the profession.

Part of the difficulty lies with the academic faculty and the different definitions of exercise physiology. Some feel that the shift means they are doing something wrong, which makes them question the new thinking by ASEP members. The reality is that they have not failed unless they choose to define exercise physiology by past thinking. Clearly, most occupations are in transition from being a discipline to a profession. Exercise physiology is no different.

While research has defined much of the success within the academic institution, exercise physiologists must now embrace the healthcare-based, professional model. Research is expected to continue as an important part of this model. In fact, it is critical to understand that the primary care model for health and wellness promotion is not in conflict with the research-publish model. Both need to be fully integrated into the new exercise physiology institution-based curriculum.

In some context, the need to shift to healthcare promotion and, therefore, disease prevention from just an emphasis on research has always existed. The missing part has been the failure of exercise physiologists to recognize the need for their own professional organization. Of course it is natural that the philosophy that associates with professionalism and professional development takes time to evolve. Now, with increased emphasis on health promotion, fitness restoration, and disease prevention or postponement, it is the task of department heads and faculty to look to the future and to plan accordingly.

Exercise Physiology: A Work in Progress

It is rarely possible to switch completely from one model to another model over night [4]. This is why it is acceptable to think of exercise physiology as work in progress. Moreover, it is the only strategy that is sensible and realistic. The ASEP leadership understands this point as well. It is purposefully built into the ASEP guidelines for accreditation standards for academic departments. Measures of accountability are consistent with measurable outcomes, but trying to be 100% specific about learning objectives and philosophical beliefs is a mistake for the time being.

All of this is another way of saying that giving shape to a new profession of healthcare practitioners takes time. Facets like course outcomes, innovative thinking, faculty development, curriculum planning, and handling anxiety and apprehension require time to be reframed in the new way of thinking. It is the logical course to take, but some will see it as illogical. The unrest that is common with change clouds the

> The healthcare model is timely, but not every exercise physiologist will agree.

thinking of some. Still other faculty members thrive on the ambiguity and flux. They enjoy the tinkering, disruption, and new ideas.

Movement to the public sector to practice exercise physiology is "the" work in progress. As mentioned, it is not easy for faculty to step away from their comfort zone of the laboratory to the community setting. This acceptance takes time to develop, too. Course content must be reframed and hands-on laboratory experiences must be redesigned to address the community-based setting.

Curriculum Changes

The reason for adding new courses and placing increased emphasis on healthcare is linked to the ASEP commitment to exercise physiology practiced in the hands of board certified exercise physiologists. In other words, the entry level degree is the undergraduate degree. This has not always been the case [5]. For decades, exercise physiology leadership and title were defined solely by the doctorate degree. It is clear that exercise physiologists with the doctorate degree are not running to the community to practice. But, while they see themselves as college professors who are primarily researchers, they understand the objective: "Teach students who believe that at graduation they will be professionally and academically prepared to practice what they have learned in school." Students today are becoming *the* exercise physiology force of the community.

Although the title has not been published before, it is appropriate to refer to these young professionals as "Community Exercise Physiologists." The focus on "community" versus "rehabilitation" sets the stage for the designation similar to "Clinical Exercise Physiologist." In actuality, however, the focus is still on the academic degree that yields, after board certification, the professional title -- Exercise Physiologist. This thinking is new and contrary to the outdated thinking of exercise specialist or fitness professional titles. Exercise physiologists now recognize the importance of change and are learning to grow and adjust with it. They are also learning to integrate information from

> **The universe is change; our life is what our thoughts make it. – Marcus Aurelius Antonius**

different disciplines that impact health and wellness. This is why the ASEP leaders are focused less on the compartmentalization by discipline and more on the integrated application to community-based priorities.

However, this thinking does present a few problems. The primary reason is that there are no plans in place to encourage students to increase their awareness of integrated knowledge. This will change. The Internet knowledge explosion is helping to change exercise physiologists who are willing to rethink the traditional approach to education. This is also why significant changes in the curriculum will be forthcoming in the not too distant future. Accessing information is important, but demonstrating the connectedness of all information is imperative. This is one of the primary goals of the ASEP leadership (i.e., to rethink the exercise physiology curriculum).

The Future

The primary vehicle for future changes and transitions in thinking may be the views that underpin the development of the

> **The goal is to keep clients healthy by engaging them in positive lifestyle changes.**

"Exercise Physiology Multidisciplinary Healthcare Clinics" [6]. There are many community-based scenarios that can be played out during the students' education in traditional laboratory experiences. This shift from traditional exercise physiology and important educational and research developments carries with it a new way of thinking that does not come easily. Change is always a challenge, especially when the emphasis is placed on the community setting.

Essential to understanding the EPMH Clinic is to know about the power that comes from being disposed to great expectations. Exercise physiologists have done great things in recent decades. But, a new philosophy has emerged with the founding of the *American Society of Exercise Physiologists* that recognizes big differences in exercise physiology. It is now no longer thought of

> **The power of expectation is great and full of reward.**

as a technician-driven discipline. It is a healthcare profession. The ASEP vision is the incentive for thinking behind the EPMH clinic-style of providing healthcare. The ASEP vision statement is also the difference between ASEP and other organizations that have not organized their philosophic framework of healthcare around academic accreditation, accountability, and the profession's scope of practice.

In many ways, the ASEP concept of healthcare should be recognize as an important step towards controlling healthcare costs. The founding of EPMH clinics will be the right step to promote healthcare and wellness. The trend in

> **The EPMH Clinic is a timely idea!**

alternative care favors this idea, particularly with respect to prevention of diseases and health promotion. Hence, the increased interest in fitness and athletics is another important reason to build EPMH clinics staffed with competent, board

200

certified professionals. The focus on keeping clients well is balanced against today's needs to continue defining the exercise physiology body of knowledge through research.

The process that drives the EPMH clinics is integrative and based on multidisciplinary data that allows for a new, personal, and alternative method of healthcare. The primary purpose is to provide high-quality, effective healthcare services to promote health and wellness. The EPMH clinics will emphasize clients first by providing cardiovascular physiology profiles using advanced technology in a scientific-based environment. It will enable exercise physiologists and other members of the EPMH team to meet the needs of the community.

Implications for Exercise Physiologists

The implications of the above growth of EPMH clinics in the future management of health, fitness, rehabilitation, and athletics is a clear mandate for ASEP to accredit more academic programs and certify more exercise physiologists. The aging "baby boomers" will have significant age-related changes in vital organs that will need functional analysis and rehabilitation. They will also have the unprecedented wealth to spend on healthcare, wellness and prevention, and the rehabilitation. Also, with money to pay fee-for-service, they stand to gain control over their healthcare decisions with increased involvement in their care.

Exercise physiologists have the

> The American public wants more involvement in their healthcare.

opportunity to organize smoking cessation programs, exercises to build athletic skills, to decrease body fat, to increase lean muscle tissue, nutritionally sound programs for athletics along with an understanding of a positive lifestyle, and to develop stress management programs to decrease stress-related conditions. The result will be an increase in the client's control over healthcare matters with a decrease in chronic disease and dysfunction.

201

Chapter Nineteen

The Entrepreneurship of Exercise Physiology

The best way to guarantee your future is to create it yourself.
– Stephen G. Haines

Many exercise physiologists have grown tired of the failed opportunities of promised jobs in the public. They are now thinking about having their own businesses. The challenge is coming to terms with what is entrepreneurship? The exercise physiology curriculum is not usually a place to study small-business management and entrepreneurship [1].

Of course, the question is: "Who will teach the business-oriented courses?" The answer is: "Exercise physiologists will teach the courses." They will teach students the mechanics of how to start entrepreneurial health, fitness, rehabilitation, and human performance businesses. Hence, in the not too distant future, with a gentle push from the ASEP leaders, students will graduate with knowledge about market economics and new market niche opportunities. They will graduate with an understanding of entrepreneurship, which is defined as the process of initiating a business venture, organizing necessary resources, and assuming the associated risks and rewards.

As the entrepreneur exercise physiologists recognize that their specialized body of knowledge is the equivalent of a business product or a healthcare service, they will get involved in the business of applied exercise physiology. Naturally, there will be financial and legal risks. There will be profits, too. Being your own boss, being in control of making decisions, and making a living as a "solo professional" are all valued outcomes. This is why

There are very real rewards of entrepreneurship.

students need information about downsizing, decentralizing, and sending out work to other firms.

None of this information is new. Today's economy is ready for exciting and creative business ideas. This is an excellent time for entrepreneurship in exercise physiology and, therefore, for new career opportunities. New businesses with increased focus on the exercise physiology body of knowledge should speed up important changes in academic courses.

Unlike the past where computer technology did not exist for the average person, exercise physiologists now have increased opportunity to integrate new technology in their overall health and physical assessments. The next step to making your dream a reality is to take the time to study business thinking and strategies. Find out what business men and women do when they start a new business venture. You can check out the Internet for this information as well. Ultimately, you will want to consult with someone who is already doing what you want to do.

The net number of new businesses created by exercise physiologists will no doubt increase dramatically during the next several decades. Among the most notable products for which exercise physiologists will be recognized as credible healthcare professionals is their "physiological niche." Virtually every application to either health or non-health issues, recreational or athletic goals, or disease or non-disease conditions will represent a new product or service. How the service is judged will depend on the credibility of exercise physiologists, and how they create and sustain their services. Of course, the stringent requirements outlined by the ASEP certification and accreditation efforts will help in many different ways.

Like most successful ventures, most original ideas that bear significant results begin in the minds of men and women who believe they can make things happen.

> **The process of letting connecting with an idea is never easy, but it is essential to moving forward.**

Their imagination creates mental pictures with details that define the desired vision and outcome.

If you really are gravitating towards exercise physiology, you have to do the research and get involved. Being an entrepreneur is no different [2]. It begins with a vision, which is likely to be a problem for exercise physiology students. No where in the curriculum or meetings is entrepreneurship taught. Visionary thinking or how to think up new ideas are not taught either. No wonder students do not have any idea about their own personal strengths or what they can do after college. This is a perfect example of a failed system.

To ASEP members, it is now abundantly clear that this problem must be corrected. The tailoring of the academic details to meet the needs of the key stakeholders (students) is taking place in selected programs of study. It is just a matter of time before others get the message that the ASEP Board of Accreditation exists. In other words, the rules and regulations that govern the undergraduate curriculum are changing, although admittedly very slow. This ASEP paradigm shift has fundamentally changed exercise physiology [3].

The business and the future of academic exercise physiology are different from the business of exercise science. The mission of exercise physiology is to educate exercise physiologists as credible (critical) thinkers with a strong applied physiology base like other established healthcare professions. Specifically, the ASEP mission is [4]:

> The *American Society of Exercise Physiologists*, the professional organization representing and promoting the profession of exercise physiology, is committed to the professional development of exercise physiology, its advancement, and the credibility of exercise physiologists.

It is clear that the mission for exercise physiology is pivotal to the design of entrepreneurial thinking. Nothing is more obvious than the work-related directions stated in the ASEP Standards of Professional Practice.

At first, the Standards may appear as everything exercise physiologists are already doing. However, with a much closer examination, it can be determined that this is not the case at all. The document defines the practice of exercise physiology beyond any document previously written. In its development, special attention was given to the importance of entrepreneurship.

These ideas rest on the assumption that exercise physiologists "practice exercise physiology" and do so within the public sector. This thinking allows for capitalizing on market leadership positions to sell exercise physiology to the public and to service a broad range of public concerns. The trick is to expand the powers of imagination, to think bigger, and to turn impossible thinking into possibility thinking. Talk about courage! The ASEP leaders have taken the initiative [5]. It is now possible make our dreams come true.

> **The concept of an "exercise physiology practice" is new.**

> **Entrepreneurship is critical to the success of all exercise physiologists.**

These are the reasons exercise physiology students should be encouraged to think in a business manner. These are the reasons professors should pursue coursework that will help their students think creatively, run with an idea, develop a business plan, locate financing, and blend exercise physiology content and laboratory skills with a market niche. These are the reasons special attention should be placed on how much money is needed, how to start a business from scratch, how to buy into an ongoing business, how to find a good accountant and attorney, how to plan for different stages of growth, how to market and promote exercise physiology as a healthcare profession.

Exercise physiologists can make a difference in healthcare. Do not ask them to be heart rate counters. Do not ask them to be happy in working part-time at the local gym. Rather, do what you can to help them network and to grow as professionals. It is possible to make the right connections that turns life around for the better. It is as straightforward a process as one could imagine. It is as simple as understanding the power within the exercise concepts and ideas that defines the profession. Then, they will know that they have created their own future.

Their power is also linked to power of believing and living the affirmations:

- We can change our thinking about exercise physiology that has been deadlocked for decades; and
- Together, if we are to get to the root of our problems and develop reasonable solutions, we must promote the educational rethinking of our undergraduate and graduate programs.

The mind-set of entrepreneurial possibilities is critical to the continued quest for change within exercise physiology and the ASEP organization [6]. Clearly, you can see that it is based on an entirely different way to think about exercise physiology. The "do nothing – keep everything as it has been" approach has resulted in doubt in students and many failed opportunities. It has set the stage for: "I can't vs. I can." And, yes, it has created problems without solutions unless exercise physiologists rethink what they are doing [7].

> Waiting for permission to begin is not characteristic of leaders. -- James M. Kouzes and Barry Z. Posner

This is why the shift towards entrepreneurial thinking is so important. It literally changes the way exercise physiologists go about solving their problems. Thus, eventually, through a combination of updated education, hands-on experiences, and ASEP leadership, the academic exercise physiologists will get the big picture. They, too, will believe this, and they, too, will think that the students need to believe it, too. Therein lies the secret to professional fulfillment as an exercise physiologist – everyone wins! Everyone needs an attitude of hopefulness, not an attitude of hopelessness. This thinking is particularly important as the ASEP leaders ask all exercise physiologists and students to think as entrepreneurs.

207

Go for It, Dream on!

Entrepreneurial thinking is defined, in part, by the idea of a dream. It begins with a new idea, new research, preparation for implementation, and then it is all about "going after the dream" [8]. Students who are thinking about exercise physiology will come to understand that exercise physiologists are very likely the key to prevention. Healthcare in America will be better once exercise physiologists are recognized as the backbone of every exercise program.

Just remember, the ASEP organization is already in motion. The beginning of the future of exercise physiology as a credible healthcare profession is well underway. To be part of the new 21st century exercise physiology, both personally and professionally, you just have to know what you want and how to get it. This book should be helpful.

Many suggestions and tips on how to begin have been made throughout the chapters to help you find your way to your dream career as an exercise physiologist. Here are some of the reasons other students wanted a career in exercise physiology:

- To be a respected and credible professional.
- To be paid at the level of a healthcare professional with medical benefits.
- No micro-management when you are the boss.
- Better appreciation of the benefits of exercise in health and athletics.
- Learn how to think as an entrepreneur.
- Look forward to going to work and finding satisfaction in helping others.
- Because the scientific (critical) thinking and research opportunities are energizing.
- To help athletes trained better.
- Healthcare is a upcoming hot career that is growing very fast.
- Areas of specialization are open with huge employment opportunities.

Chapter Twenty

New Partnerships

The dogmas of the quiet past are inadequate to the stormy present. The occasion is piled high with difficulty, and we must rise to the occasion. As our case is new, so we must think and act anew. – Lincoln, 1862

Whether we choose to believe it or not, we are living in a time with incredible healthcare problems. Each year, the issues and concerns that surround healthcare get worse. And, frankly, according to some experts in the field, society is on the verge of a collapse in healthcare funding. The increases in healthcare costs are over the edge. It is not clear whether or not anything will emerge to change the course of spending, yet something must change. Increasingly, more Americans are pessimistic about the future of healthcare, and they know that it will only get worse if something is not done quickly.

From the exercise physiologist's perspective, part of the change process is to take inventory of "exercise as medicine." Indeed, future generations are likely to judge exercise physiologists on just how successful they were in building the professional relationships and collaborative partnerships with nurses, physical therapists, physicians and others in the

To be sure, exercise physiology is developing as a force to be understood and applied in healthcare.

health field. What is obvious is this: It is unacceptable to stay as we have been. The proverbial "you know what" has finally hit the fan. Exercise physiologists can do better. Other healthcare professionals can do better, too. All the evidence supports the importance of collaboration and new partnerships to lower healthcare costs that will benefit the public.

This is why the leaders of the *American Society of Exercise Physiologists* have encouraged the update of academic programs and have designed a credible board certification. They believe that healthcare professionals should collaborate by sharing responsibility and knowledge. But, the truth is, exercise physiologists are only just beginning their healthcare journey. To date, what has been done within the context of ASEP is short of a miracle [1]. The results have contributed significantly to the professional development of exercise physiology, but much more must be done.

Exercise is at the center of important changes in the human body, both anatomically and physiologically. And, despite the fact that regular exercise is under-used by Americans, the benefits are not in doubt. Now, more than ever, exercise physiologists need leaders who are willing to build partnerships with a shared purpose to strengthen the quality of life of all Americans. The face of the nation is aging. No longer is the issue just the prevention of disease. Now the continuation of a quality oriented life is at the forefront of the nation's concerns. The opportunity to live a longer life is a reality that is not independent of scientifically-based principles and disciplines. A variety of practice settings and new software options to assess and communicate more effectively with clients await tomorrow's exercise physiologists.

Setting the Stage for Change and Collaboration
The purpose of this chapter is to stretch the reader's thinking and to visualize career opportunities beyond what is presently tracked by different sources. Hence, it should not come as a surprise that linking exercise physiology with the established healthcare professions is expected to be a big part of the new healthcare system. It is also encouraging to note that, to a minor degree, the alliance to collaborative principles of relationships and shared decision-making between established healthcare professions and exercise physiology is already a reality.

> Collaboration is both a process and an outcome in which shared interest or conflict that cannot be addressed by any single individual is addressed by key stakeholders. – Mary Follett and B. Gray

Therefore, as more healthcare professionals learn of the new exercise physiology, success in stable and financially viable careers is increasingly assured. The 21st century exercise physiologist will gradually move towards the delivery of healthcare through increased physiological measurements [2]. The movement will be assisted by the development and use of new and innovative laboratory technology and software in the assessment and delivery of more comprehensive and detailed care.

In fact, this is exactly why it is important to look beyond the immediate view of exercise physiology. It is not, for example, a discipline driven to help athletes run faster and get stronger. While these are important goals, they are very narrow in perspective. Just think of the career opportunities in the following areas:

- Pediatrics
- Obesity
- Musculoskeletal weakness/dysfunction
- Blood lipids
- Depression
- Aging
- Cancer

The differences between the 20th and 21st century exercise physiologist will be both collaborative and technological. Both will increase career opportunities and the professional career niche defined by the ASEP exercise physiologists. Much of the work during the recent decades in regards to cardiopulmonary rehabilitation jobs will remain essentially unchanged. The infrastructure for direct involvement and continued management of cardiopulmonary patients is well developed. But, the distribution of exercise physiologists throughout the healthcare system will increase in most of the areas mentioned above. This will help to improve patient outcomes along with significant improvements in employment opportunities.

Aside from the expectation that exercise physiologists will develop their own multidisciplinary healthcare clinics, much of exercise physiology will be practiced alongside medical doctors, nurses, dietitians, physical therapists, and other healthcare professionals. Established professionals will open their doors to board certified exercise physiologists. Those who can foresee these challenges and respond to them accordingly and creatively will have a huge professional edge over those who remain indifferent.

> Breaking the chains of our control myths and freeing ourselves from the bondage of bad leaders both move us along an important path.
> -- Jean Lipman-Blumen

Recognized as experts in cardiovascular rehabilitation and musculoskeletal assessment, exercise physiologists will find comfort and security in interdisciplinary collaboration with other healthcare professionals. Also, as they learn to manage the new paradigm in healthcare, there will be an increase in career responsibilities on all members of the profession. They will become increasingly engaged in new and innovative ways to handle the screening, tracking, and referring of high-risk patients to other professionals.

The implication of the paradigm shift from fitness instructor to healthcare professional is that exercise is medicine and that the exercise prescription should to be written by the exercise physiologist.

The high-tech and computerized equipment of the exercise physiologist will drive the health prevention and rehabilitation strategies. It will continue to be an evidence-based practice, meaning that assessment, rehabilitation, and care is based on scientific principles. The exercise physiologists in the established healthcare environments will have increased access to technological resources and cost-effective quality care. Yet, they will seek newer and innovative ways of stabilizing and improving health of their clients.

The impact of the technology and the partnerships will result in the increased acceptance of exercise physiology into the family of healthcare professionals. The collaboration of more healthcare professionals will enhance public health by prevention, early detection, and the reduction of morbidity from chronic diseases. The expansion of professional responsibilities of exercise physiologists of the future in areas of providing cost effective and technologically appropriate care, promoting healthy lifestyles through consultation and counseling, helping clients and patients think critically about prevention, personal and family accountability for health matters, and healthcare decision-making in regards to the benefits of regular exercise and athletics, and guiding patients with spiritual and sociological issues and concerns are expected services.

Exercise physiologists will help ensure the continuity of care in partnership with medical doctors and other alternative physicians in private practice. They will hire exercise physiologists as members of their healthcare team. The inevitability of this occurrence is a function of the power of regular exercise. There is little doubt that exercise is medicine, and that the practice of exercise physiology has reached a significant turning point with the medical community's understanding of this point. This is why exercise physiologists can expect the eager involvement of the medical community. Together, they will build intra-organizational levels of collaboration.

The advantages of the partnership, whether it is with the medical doctor or the dentist or even the dietitian (all in private practice) is an increase in collective power and influence in healthcare matters. Members of the partnership will understand the importance of a shared vision with the objective larger than any one interest group.

> **Shared decision making is one of the hallmark dimensions of collaborative practice. – Deborah B. Gardner**

The agenda is one of the absolute best-care for the common good of the client (patient). It is with the greatest confidence that exercise physiologists will continue to meet the needs of the profession and those of their clients.

> The real world is simply too terrible to admit; it tells man that he is a small, trembling animal who will decay and die. Illusion changes all this, makes man seem important, vital to the universe, immortal in some way. The masses look to the leaders to give them just the untruth that they need; the leader continues the illusions and magnifies them into a truly heroic victory. -- Ernest Becker

213

Partnerships with positive collaboration strengthen networking opportunities, which helps everyone involved. Also important, members of different professions have increased resources to support and commit to solving healthcare problems. The sense of a shared mission or vision will help to drive the success of collaborative efforts and partnerships. In the end, the public will benefit in better healthcare with less overall costs.

References

Chapter 1

1. *American Society of Exercise Physiologists.* (2006). Home Page. [Online]. http://www.asep.org
2. *American Society of Exercise Physiologists.* (2006). ASEP Standards of Professional Practice. [Online]. http://www.asep.org/standards.htm

Chapter 2

1. *American Society of Exercise Physiologists.* (2006). The EPC Exam. [Online]. http://faculty.css.edu/tboone2/asep/ASEPcertification.html
2. Astorino, T.A., Robergs, R.A.,Ghiasvand, F., Marks, D., and Burns, S. (2000). Incidence of the Oxygen Plateau at VO_2 max during Exercise Testing to Volitional Fatigue. *Journal of Exercise Physiologyonline.* 3:4:1-12. [Online]. http://www.asep.org/Documents/Astorin1.doc

Chapter 3

1. Durak, E. (2004). How Exercise Physiologists can Maneuver into a Solid Health Care Niche with Bariatric Patients. *Professionalization of Exercise Physiologyonline.* 7:7 [Online]. http://faculty.css.edu/tboone2/asep/ExercisePhysiologyBariatricHealthcare Niche.html
2. *American Society of Exercise Physiologists.* (2006). Career Opportunities in Exercise Physiology. [Online]. http://www.asep.org/career.htm
3. *Boone, T.* (2004). The Professional Practice of Exercise Physiology and Ethical Thinking. *Professionalization of Exercise Physiologyonline.* 7:2 [Online]. http://faculty.css.edu/tboone2/asep/ProfessionalPracticeANDethicalTHIN KING.html

Chapter 4

1. American Society of Exercise Physiologists. (2006). Board of Directors. [Online]. http://www.asep.org/execbod.htm
2. Boone, T. (2002). Critical Thinking: A New Day Dawning in Exercise Physiology. *Professionalization of Exercise Physiologyonline.* 5:11 [Online]. http://faculty.css.edu/tboone2/asep/ExercisePhysiologyCRITICALThinkin g.html

3. Boone, T. (2001). *Professional Development of Exercise Physiology.* Lewiston, NY: The Edwin Mellen Press.

Chapter 5

1. *American Society of Exercise Physiologists.* (2006). Home Page. [Online]. http://www.asep.org
2. *American Academy of Kinesiology and Physical Education.* (2006). Home Page. [Online]. http://www.aakpe.org/
3. *American Society of Exercise Physiologists.* (2006). Code of Ethics. [Online]. http://www.asep.org/ethics.htm
4. *American College of Sports Medicine.* (2006). Home Page. [Online]. http://www.acsm.org//AM/Template.cfm?Section=Home_Page
5. *American Association of Cardiovascular and Pulmonary Rehabilitation.* (2006). Home Page. [Online]. http://www.aacvpr.org/
6. *American Society of Exercise Physiologists.* (2006). Home/Archive Page. [Online]. http://www.asep.org/jeponline/JEPhome.php
7. *American Society of Exercise Physiologists.* (2006). Home Page. [Online]. http://faculty.css.edu/tboone2/asep/Professionalization.html
8. *The Center for Exercise Physiology-online.* (2006). Home Page. [Online]. http://www.exercisephysiologists.com/
9. The Center for Exercise Physiology-online. (2006). Journal of Professional Exercise Physiology. [Online]. http://www.exercisephysiologists.com/JournalofProfessionalExercisePhysiology/index.html
10. Boone, T. (2005). *Exercise Physiology: Professional Issues, Organizational Concerns, and Ethical Trends.* Lewiston, NY: The Edwin Mellen Press.

Chapter 6

1. Boone, T. (2006). Shouldn't We be Concerned about Performance-Enhancing Substances? *Journal of Professional Exercise Physiology.* 4:1 [Online]. http://www.exercisephysiologists.com/JPEPJan2006PES/index.html
2. *American Society of Exercise Physiologists.* (2006). Board Certified Exercise Physiologists. [Online]. http://faculty.css.edu/tboone2/asep/ASEPBoardCertifiedMembers.html
3. *Ergonomics, Inc.* (2006). Ask the Ergonomist. [Online]. http://www.ergoinc.com/Ask_the_Ergonomist.htm
4. *Health Professions Network.* (2006). Exercise Physiology. [Online]. http://www.healthpronet.org/ahp_month/08_04.html
5. *Wellcoaches.* (2006). Wellcoach Home Page. [Online]. http://www.wellcoach.com/

Chapter 7

1. *Career Planning.About* (2006). How Do I Choose the Right Career? [Online].
   http://careerplanning.about.com/cs/choosingacareer/f/right_career.htm
2. *The Job Market.* (2003). A Five-Step Career Plan. [Online].
   http://www.thejobmarket.org/jobseekers/choose_steps.asp
3. *The College of St. Scholastica.* (2006). Exercise Physiology. [Online].
   http://www.css.edu/x1464.xml
4. *Lifestyle Management.* (2006). Home Page. [Online].
   http://www.lifestylemanagement.net/index.htm
5. *Guidant Corporation.* (2006). Home Page. [Online].
   http://www.mnfcpug.org/GuidantCorporation.php
6. *Arete Healthfit.* (2006). Home Page. [Online]. http://aretehealthfit.com/
7. *LifeTime Fitness.* (2006). Home Page. [Online].
   http://www.lifetimefitness.com/clubs/index.cfm?strWebAction=area_map
   &intMarketAreaId=1
8. *Cardiovascular Consultants.* (2006). Improving Patient's Health One Beat at a Time. [Online]. http://www.northcardiology.com/
9. *White Bear Racket and Swim.* (2006). Home Page. [Online].
   http://www.wbfit.com/
10. *Rehabilitation Institute of Chicago.* (2006). Home Page. [Online].
    http://www.ric.org/
11. *National Strength and Conditioning Association.* (2006). Home Page. [Online]. http://www.nsca-lift.org/
12. *USA Weightlifting.* (2006). Home Page. [Online].
    http://www.msbn.tv/usavision/
13. *The College of St. Scholastica.* (2006). Graduate Exercise Physiology Home Page. [Online]. http://www.css.edu/x2111.xml
14. *St. Joseph's Hospital.* (2006). Cardiac Rehabilitation. [Online].
    http://www.sjbhealth.org/12889.cfm
15. *Winston-Salem State University.* (2006). School of Education and Human Performance. [Online].
    http://www.wssu.edu/WSSU/UndergraduateStudies/School+of+Education
16. *University of Minnesota.* (2006). Graduate School – Kinesiology. [Online]. http://www.catalogs.umn.edu/grad/programs/g102.html
17. *Wolfe-Harris Center for Clinical Studies.* (2006). Home Page. [Online]. http://nwhealth.edu/research/WHCCS/index.html

Chapter 8

1. *National Association of Colleges and Employers.* (2003). NACE Salary Survey. Job Choices in Business. 46th edition.

2. *ExerciseCareers.com.* (2006). Home Page. [Online].
   http://www.exercisecareers.com/
3. *Exercisejobs.*com. (2006). Home Page. [Online].
   http://www.exercisejobs.com/
4. *Health and Wellness Jobs.com.* (2006). Home Page. [Online].
   http://www.healthandwellnessjobs.com/
5. *HPCareer.net.* (2006). Hope Page. [Online].
   http://www.hpcareer.net/hpc/redesign/index.html

Chapter 9

1. Jungbauer, S. (2003). Values and Beliefs: A Lesson Learned.
   Professionalization of Exercise Physiologyonline. 6:11 [Online].
   http://faculty.css.edu/tboone2/asep/ValuesANDbeliefs.html
2. Boone, T. (2003). Values Clarification in Exercise Physiology.
   Professionalization of Exercise Physiologyonline.
   http://faculty.css.edu/tboone2/asep/ValuesClarificationANDExercisePhysi
   ology.html 6:6 [Online].
3. Pittsley, J. and Riley, P. (2000). Meeting the Standards of a Profession.
   Professionalization of Exercise Physiologyonline. 3:8 [Online].
   http://faculty.css.edu/tboone2/asep/Standards.html
4. Boone, T. (2000). The Passionate Pursuit of Professionalism: A Critical
   Analysis. *Professionalization of Exercise Physiologyonline.* 3:10 [Online].
   http://faculty.css.edu/tboone2/asep/Passionate.html
5. Russo, J.V. (200 Exercise as Medication: An Exercise Physiologist's
   View. *Professionalization of Exercise Physiologyonline.* 5:1 [Online].
   http://faculty.css.edu/tboone2/asep/PEPonlineJan2002ExerciseAsMedicati
   on.html
6. Boone, T. (2002). Exercise is Therapy, Prevention, and Treatment: An
   Exercise Physiologist's Perspective. *Professionalization of Exercise
   Physiologyonline.* 5:3 [Online].
   http://faculty.css.edu/tboone2/asep/ExerciseIsTherapy.html

Chapter 10

1. Boone, T. (2002). Exercise is Therapy, Prevention, and Treatment: An
   Exercise Physiologist's Perspective. *Professionalization of Exercise
   Physiologyonline.* 5:3 [Online].
   http://faculty.css.edu/tboone2/asep/ExerciseIsTherapy.html
2. Robergs, R.A. and Roberts, S.O. (1997). *Exercise Physiology: Exercise,
   Performance, and Clinical Applications.* St. Louis, Missouri: Mosby.
3. Swain, D.P. and Leutholtz, B.C. (2002). *Exercise Prescription.*
   Champaign, IL: Human Kinetics Publishers, Inc.

4. Drake, R.L., Vogl, W., and Mitchell, A.W.M. (2005). *Gray's Anatomy for Students*. Philadelphia, PA: Elsevier Inc.
5. Oatis, C.A. (2004]. *Kinesiology: The Mechanics and Pathomechanics of Human Movement*. Philadelphia, PA: Lippincott Williams and Wilkins.
6. American Association of Cardiovascular and Pulmonary Rehabilitation. (1995). *Guidelines for Cardiac Rehabilitation Programs*. Champaign, IL: Human Kinetics Publishers, Inc.
7. Ellestad, M.H. (1996). *Stress Testing: Principles and Practice*. Edition 4. Philadelphia, PA: F.A. Davis Company
8. Astrand, P-O, Rodahl, K. Dahl, H.A., and Stromme, S.B. (2003). *Textbook of Work Physiology: Physiological Bases of Exercise*. Champaign, IL: Human Kinetics Publishers, Inc.
9. Wildman, R. and Miller, B. (2004). *Sports and Fitness Nutrition*. Belmont, CA: Wadsworth/Thomson.
10. Pollock, M.L. and Wilmore, J.H. (1990). *Exercise in Health and Disease: Evaluation and Prescription for Prevention and Rehabilitation*. Second Edition. Philadelphia, PA: W.B. Saunders Company.
11. Hyllegard, R., Mood, D.P., and Morrow, J.R. (1996). *Interpreting Research in Sport and Exercise Science*. St. Louis, Missouri: Mosby.
12. Rice, V.H. (2000). *Handbook of Stress, Coping, and Health: Implications for Nursing Research, Theory, and Practice*. Thousand Oaks, CA: Sage Publications, Inc.

Chapter 11

1. Birnbaum, L. and Hedlund, C. (1998). The Oxygen Cost of Walking With an Artifically Immobilized Knee With and Without a Shoe-Lift. *Journal of Exercise Physiologyonline*. 1:1 [Online].
http://faculty.css.edu/tboone2/asep/jan2.htm
2. Boone, T. and DeWeese, J. (1998). The Effect of Psychophysiologic Self-Regulation on Running Economy. *Journal of Exercise Physiologyonline* . 1:1 [Online]. http://faculty.css.edu/tboone2/asep/jan6.htm
3. Redondo, D. and Boone, T. (1998). Central and Peripheral Circulatory Responses during Four Different Recovery Positions Immediately Following Submaximal Exercise. *Journal of Exercise Physiologyonline*. *1:1*

Chapter 12

1. *American Society of Exercise Physiologists*. (2006). Standards of Professional Practice. [Online]. http://www.asep.org/standards.htm
2. *American Society of Exercise Physiologists*. (2006). Guidelines for Undergraduate Accreditation. [Online] http://www.asep.org/accreditation/

3. *American Society of Exercise Physiologists*. (2006). Exercise Physiology Accredited Programs. [Online]. http://www.asep.org/programs.htm
4. *Robergs, R.* (2006). Personal Home Page. [Online]. http://www.unm.edu/~rrobergs/

Chapter 13

1. *American Society of Exercise Physiologists*. (2006). Guidelines for the EPC Candidate. [Online]. http://faculty.css.edu/tboone2/asep/ASEPcertification.html
2. Skinner, J.S. (1987). *Exercise Testing and Exercise Prescription for Special Cases: Theoretical Basis and Clinical Application*. Philadelphia, PA: Lea and Febiger.
3. Boone, T. (2003). The COURAGE to QUESTION What is Exercise Physiology in the 21st Century. *Professionalization of Exercise Physiologyonline*. 6:1 [Online]. http://faculty.css.edu/tboone2/asep/COURAGEtoQUESTION.html

Chapter 14

1. *Commission of Accreditation of Allied Health Education Programs*. (2006). Home Page. [Online]. http://www.caahep.org/
2. *Board of Certification for the Athletic Trainer*. (2006). Home Page. [Online]. http://www.bocatc.org/

Chapter 15

1. Boone, T. (2005). *Exercise Physiology: Professional Issues, Organizational Concerns, and Ethical Trends*. Lewiston, NY: The Edwin Mellen Press.

Chapter 16

1. *American Society of Exercise Physiologists*. (2006). Code of Ethics. [Online]. http://www.asep.org/ethics.htm
2. Boone, T. (2005). On Becoming an Exercise Physiologist. *Professionalization of Exercise Physiologyonline*. 8:2 [Online]. http://faculty.css.edu/tboone2/asep/OnBecomingAnExercisePhysiologist.html
3. Hall, M. (2004). Believing in ASEP is Important. *Professionalization of Exercise Physiologyonline*. 7:2 [Online]. http://faculty.css.edu/tboone2/asep/BelievingInASEPisIMPORTANT.html
4. Boone, T. (2003). The Role of ASEP in the Professional Development of Exercise Physiology. *Professionalization of Exercise Physiologyonline*.

6:6 [Online].
http://faculty.css.edu/tboone2/asep/ProfessionalDevelopmentOfExerciseP
hysiology.html

5. Boone, T. (2004). The Courage to Create the Future. *Professionalization of Exercise Physiologyonline*. 7:9 [Online].
http://faculty.css.edu/tboone2/asep/CourageToCreate.html

6. Boone, T. (2005). Niche Marketing: The Exercise Physiologist's Point of View. *Professionalization of Exercise Physiologyonline*. 8:9 [Online].
http://faculty.css.edu/tboone2/asep/NicheMarketingTheExercisePhysiologi
stPointOfView.html

Chapter 17

1. Boone, T. (2004). Exercise Physiologists as Educators and Healthcare Practitioners in the Multidisciplinary Exercise Physiology Healthcare (MEPH) Clinic. *Professionalization of Exercise Physiologyonline*. 7:1 [Online].
http://faculty.css.edu/tboone2/asep/MultidisciplinaryExercisePhysiologyH
ealthcareClinic.html

Chapter 18

1. Boone, T. (2004). The ASEP Exercise Physiologist: Leadership and Shared Expectations. *Professionalization of Exercise Physiologyonline*. 7:1 [Online].
http://faculty.css.edu/tboone2/asep/ExercisePhysiologySharedExpectation
s.html

2. Boone, T. (2000). The Exercise Physiology Core Curriculum. *Professionalization of Exercise Physiologyonline*. 3:6 [Online].
http://faculty.css.edu/tboone2/asep/CoreCurriculum.html

3. Kaelin, M.E. (2000). Building a Future for All Exercise Physiologists. *Professionalization of Exercise Phyysiologists*. 3:5 [Online].
http://faculty.css.edu/tboone2/asep/BuildingExercisePhysiology.html

4. Boone, T. (2001). Taking Responsibility for Professionalism. *Professionalization of Exercise Physiologyonline*. 4:2 [Online].
http://faculty.css.edu/tboone2/asep/TakingRESPONSIBILITY.html

5. Boone, T. (2002). The Psychocultural Science of Taking Responsibility. *Professionalization of Exercise Physiologyonline*. 5:8 [Online].
http://faculty.css.edu/tboone2/asep/PsychoculturalSCIENCE.html

6. Boone, T. (2004). Exercise Physiologists as Educators and Healthcare Practitioners in the Multidisciplinary Exercise Physiology Healthcare (MEPH) Clinic. *Professionalization of Exercise Physiologyonline*. 7:1 [Online].

http://faculty.css.edu/tboone2/asep/MultidisciplinaryExercisePhysiologyH
ealthcareClinic.html

Chapter 19

1. Boone, T. (2003). The Entrepreneurship of Exercise Physiology. *Professionalization of Exercise Physiologyonline*. 6:3 [Online]. http://faculty.css.edu/tboone2/asep/EntrepreneurshipOfExercisePhysiolog y.html
2. Daugherty, S. (2005). Entrepreneuring as an Exercise Physiologist. *Professionalization of Exercise Physiologyonline*. 8:4 [Online]. http://faculty.css.edu/tboone2/asep/Entrepreneuring.html
3. Boone, T. (2005). Birds of a Feather Flock Together. *Professionalization of Exercise Physiologyonline*. 8:9 [Online]. http://faculty.css.edu/tboone2/asep/BirdsOfaFeatherFlockTogether.html
4. Boone, T. (2005). Managing the Organization: Understanding Vision and Mission Statements. *Professionalization of Exercise Physiologyonline*. 8:5 [Online]. http://faculty.css.edu/tboone2/asep/ManagingTheOrganization.html
5. Boone, T. (2005). The Science of Leadership. *Professionalization of Exercise Physiologyonline*. 8:5 [Online]. http://faculty.css.edu/tboone2/asep/SCIENCEofLEADERSHIP.html
6. Boone, T. (2006). The Will to be an Exercise Physiologist. [Online]. http://www.boonethink.com/
7. Boone, T. (2002). The Power and Influence of Beliefs. *Professionalization of Exercise Physiologyonline*. 5:7 [Online]. http://faculty.css.edu/tboone2/asep/ExercisePhysiologyBeliefs.html
8. Boone. T. (2005). Dare to Dream: Boldness has Magic! *Professionalization of Exercise Physiologyonline*. 8:5 [Online]. http://faculty.css.edu/tboone2/asep/DareToDream.html

Chapter 20

1. Boone, T. (2003). The ASEP Organization is a Paradigm Shift. *Professionalization of Exercise Physiologyonline*. 6:2 [Online]. http://faculty.css.edu/tboone2/asep/TheASEPparadigmShift.html
2. Boone, T. (2005). *Exercise Physiology: Professional Issues, Organizational Concerns, and Ethical Trends*. Lewiston, NY: The Edwin Mellen Press.

Index